Praise for Paramahansa Yogananda's commentary on the Bhagavad Gita...

God Talks With Arjuna: The Bhagavad Gita—
A New Translation and Commentary

(published by Self-Realization Fellowship, 1995)

"Yogananda's commentary penetrates to the heart of the Bhagavad Gita to reveal the deep spiritual and psychological truths lying at the heart of this great Hindu text."—*Publishers Weekly*

"One of the finest works on the subject...a masterpiece of spiritual, literary and philosophical work."—*India Post*

"This lavish two-volume edition...is a delight for the eye and the heart...a testimony to [Yogananda's] extraordinary understanding, springing from direct experience of the higher realities, and also his compassion for seekers thirsting for spiritual truth....Experience the true pulse of the Bhagavad Gita and be pulled into its sphere of influence through the luminous words of one of this century's great yoga masters."—*Yoga Journal*

"A flower of great beauty has risen from the writings and tradition of Paramahansa Yogananda...he brings the Bhagavad Gita into immediate focus for modern times....Most highly recommended!"—*Leading Edge Review*

"This monumental translation and commentary on the Bhagavad Gita, by one of India's illustrious saints, breaks new ground....Yogananda explores the science of yoga encrypted in the Gita...and the way this ancient discipline makes possible the direct experience of God. In simple but eloquent language, he sets forth a sweeping chronicle."—*The Quest*

"Each verse is meticulously translated by Yogananda, but it is [his] explanations drawing on a vast array of knowledge that is the main attraction here.... An impressive panorama of wisdom, of psychology, spirit, epistemology, physiology and yoga doctrine...Stunning."—*The Book Reader*

"[Yogananda's] commentary...reveals the highest truth, yet remains accessible to all seekers by its immediacy and simplicity of expression....What [his] *Autobiography* achieves in the realm of human experience, *God Talks With Arjuna* achieves as a complete teaching for the spiritual life....This is a book that one can study and cherish for a lifetime. It will be remembered as one of the great commentaries on the Gita...."—*Yoga International*

Paramahansa Yogananda (1893–1952)

THE
YOGA
OF THE
BHAGAVAD
GITA

*An Introduction to
India's Universal Science
of God-Realization*

Selections from the writings of
Paramahansa Yogananda

Self-Realization Fellowship
FOUNDED 1920
Paramahansa Yogananda

Authorized by the International Publications Council of Self-Realization Fellowship

The Self-Realization Fellowship name and emblem (shown above) appear on all SRF books, recordings, and other publications, assuring the reader that a work originates with the society established by Paramahansa Yogananda and faithfully conveys his teachings.

CIP data has been applied for.

ISBN-13: 978-0-87612-033-0
Printed in the United States of America
1731-J700

Front cover illustration:
Bhagavan Krishna as Yogeshwara, "Lord of Yoga"

Contents

PART 2: The Bhagavad Gita *(translation by Paramahansa Yogananda)*

Preface

"Sri Krishna's message in the Bhagavad Gita is the perfect answer for the modern age, and any age: Yoga of dutiful action, of nonattachment, and of meditation for God-realization. To work without the inner peace of God is Hades; and to work with His joy ever bubbling through the soul is to carry a portable paradise within, wherever one goes."

—Paramahansa Yogananda

For centuries, the Bhagavad Gita has been regarded as one of the very greatest expressions of the universal spiritual wisdom that is the unifying legacy of all humanity. It is India's most beloved scripture of yoga, the science of divine communion—and a timeless prescription for happiness and balanced success in everyday life.

Numerous translations of the Bhagavad Gita have been made from the original Sanskrit into English and other European languages—some by linguists or scholars of philosophy, others by literary figures, many by spiritual teachers or yogis. Among the well-known translations in English, some readers have enjoyed the more poetic renderings (such as that of Sir Edwin Arnold, for example); other versions are noteworthy for their literal presentation and linguistic analysis of the Sanskrit terminology.

What distinguishes the original translation by Paramahansa Yogananda is that, for the first time, the English rendering was done with an understanding of the profound inner symbology hidden in the Sanskrit verses—symbology which, rightly understood, reveals previously undisclosed depths in the Gita as a consummate guidebook to the science of yoga and the art of spiritual living in the material world.

In its own words, the Gita is described as "the scripture of yoga and the science of God-realization" (*brahmavidyāyām yogaśāstre*). Yogananda's translation eminently fulfills the promise of this description, as

well as revealing the Gita's consonance with the other ancient masterpiece on yoga, the *Yoga Sutras* of Patanjali.

The historical battle portrayed in the Bhagavad Gita, he states, is an
allegory of the inner conflict between man's base materialistic instincts
and his innate yearning to attain the blissful spiritual consciousness of
oneness with the Divine. "In support of this analogy," he writes, "there
is shown an exact correspondence between the material and spiritual
attributes of man as described by Patanjali in his *Yoga Sutras* and the
warring contestants cited in the Gita."

In addition to the symbology hidden in the Sanskrit names of the
principal characters, an understanding of many spiritual terms and con-
cepts pertinent to yoga is implicit in the original Sanskrit of the verses.
These would have been automatically understood by the sages who
passed the Gita's wisdom down the ages, and their disciples—even
though not specifically mentioned in the wording of a given verse. To
facilitate an accurate and complete understanding of the ancient Sanskrit
verses by modern readers, Paramahansa Yogananda incorporated these
implicit meanings in his translation and in the related commentary.

To accomplish a translation that is fully expressive of the intent of
the Gita's author surely requires that the translator have a personal, ex-
periential realization of the profound truths and high states of spiritual
consciousness that the Gita elucidates. Paramahansa Yogananda, author
of the spiritual classic *Autobiography of a Yogi* and justly celebrated as
"the Father of Yoga in the West," was uniquely qualified to penetrate the
deepest meanings of the Gita. Recognized worldwide as a God-knowing
sage of the highest degree, he was also the chosen representative of a renowned lineage of divinely illumined masters: his own guru, Swami Sri
Yukteswar (1855–1936); his guru's guru, Lahiri Mahasaya of Banaras
(1828–1895); and the supreme guru in the line, Mahavatar Babaji. In
the modern renaissance of India's timeless spiritual heritage that has had
such a profound impact on global civilization, these four masters played
a preeminent role—reviving for the present age the highest meditation
techniques of yoga, which had been known and taught in India's ancient
spiritual civilization but had been lost to humanity at large for centuries
during the Dark Ages. Paramahansaji wrote:

"My guru and *paramgurus*—Swami Sri Yukteswar, Lahiri Maha-saya, and Mahavatar Babaji—are *rishis* of this present age, mas-ters who themselves are God-realized living scriptures. They have bequeathed to the world—along with the long-lost scientific tech-nique of *Kriya Yoga**—a new revelation of the holy Bhagavad Gita, relevant primarily to the science of yoga and to *Kriya Yoga* in particular."

It was these great masters who entrusted to Paramahansa Yogananda the task of teaching the Gita's innermost wisdom and essence of yoga worldwide. His guru, Swami Sri Yukteswar, said to him: "You perceive all the truth of the Bhagavad Gita....Go and give that revealed truth with your interpretations: a new scripture will be born."†

What Is Yoga, Really?

Though many people think of yoga only as physical exercises—the *asanas* or postures that have gained widespread popularity in recent decades—these are actually only the most superficial aspect of this pro-found science of unfolding the infinite potentials of the human mind and soul.

The word *yoga* itself means "union": of the individual consciousness or soul with the Universal Consciousness or Spirit. There are various paths of Yoga that lead toward this goal, each one a specialized branch of one comprehensive system:

Hatha Yoga—a system of physical postures, or *asanas*, whose higher purpose is to purify the body, giving one awareness and control over its internal states and rendering it fit for meditation.

---

* "*Kriya* is an ancient science," Yogananda wrote in his *Autobiography of a Yogi*. "Lahiri Mahasaya received it from his great guru, Babaji, who rediscovered and clarified the technique after it had been lost in the Dark Ages. Babaji renamed it, simply, *Kriya Yoga*."

"The *Kriya Yoga* that I am giving to the world through you in this nineteenth century," Babaji told Lahiri Mahasaya, "is a revival of the same science that Krishna gave millenniums ago to Arjuna; and that was later known to Patanjali and Christ, and to St. John, St. Paul, and other dis-ciples." *Kriya Yoga* is taught to students of the *Self-Realization Fellowship Lessons* who fulfill the requirements of certain preliminary spiritual disciplines. See page 165.

† Paramahansa Yogananda's comprehensive work on the Gita is titled *God Talks With Arjuna: The Bhagavad Gita—Royal Science of God-Realization* (two volumes; published by Self-Realization Fellowship, Los Angeles).

Karma Yoga—selfless service to others as part of one's larger Self, without attachment to the results; and the performance of all actions with the consciousness of God as the Doer.

Mantra Yoga—centering the consciousness within through *japa*, or the repetition of certain universal root-word sounds representing a particular aspect of Spirit.

Bhakti Yoga—all-surrendering devotion through which one strives to see and love the divinity in every creature and in everything, thus maintaining an unceasing worship.

Jnana Yoga (pronounced "Gyana Yoga")—the path of wisdom, which emphasizes the application of discriminative intelligence to achieve spiritual liberation.

Raja Yoga—the royal or highest path of Yoga, formally systematized in the second century B.C. by the Indian sage Patanjali, which combines the essence of all the other paths.

At the heart of the Raja Yoga system, balancing and unifying these various approaches, is the practice of definite, scientific methods of meditation—such as Kriya Yoga—that enable one to perceive, from the very beginning of one's efforts, glimpses of the ultimate goal—conscious union with the inexhaustibly blissful Spirit.

The Bhagavad Gita shows how each of the various paths of yoga contributes to the overall goal: union with God.* Karma Yoga, Bhakti Yoga, and Jnana Yoga (Sankhya) are each the subject of one of the Gita's eighteen chapters, and are also referred to in other verses throughout the text. (For example, Jnana Yoga, the path of discriminative wisdom, is inherent in the entire story, in that the Gita's heros—the Pandavas—symbolize the enlightened powers of discrimination that the soul must awaken to attain liberation.) The other principal yoga paths mentioned above are likewise included in the Gita's comprehen-

---

* That Jesus also knew and taught the same universal science of God-realization and precepts for spiritual living is shown in a companion volume to the present book: *The Yoga of Jesus: Understanding the Hidden Teachings of the Gospels*—excerpts from Paramahansa Yogananda's highly acclaimed two-volume commentary on the original teachings of Jesus, *The Second Coming of Christ: The Resurrection of the Christ Within You.*

sive teaching and elucidated in Paramahansaji's commentary.

Combining the separate approaches into a balanced, comprehensive path to the highest spiritual consciousness, the Gita can indeed be considered a preeminent scripture on Raja Yoga: "the royal science of God-realization," as Paramahansa Yogananda subtitled his two-volume commentary, *God Talks With Arjuna*. In that work, each Gita verse is followed by an in-depth explanation of its spiritual meaning and practical application in daily life. In this present book, his translation alone—without interspersed commentary—is published sequentially for the first time.

The excerpts from Paramahansaji's comprehensive commentary that are included in this present work focus on the beginning of the Gita discourse—giving a glimpse of the spiritual symbolism represented by the key figures in the two warring armies.* This introductory explanation is then followed (in Part II) by the 700 Gita verses in uninterrupted sequence. Having in mind the allegorical key provided in the first part of this book, the reader will easily be able to understand the intent of Lord Krishna throughout the eighteen chapters of Gita dialogue: to arouse his disciple Arjuna (and every spiritual seeker) to overthrow the usurping psychological forces of the body-bound ego and material ignorance and reclaim his eternal spiritual identity, one with Spirit.

A brief work such as the present one can provide only an introductory glimpse of the profound and inspiring depths encapsulated in the Gita's concise text—depths that are fully unveiled by Paramahansa Yogananda's profound commentary on each of the verses, as presented in the two volumes of *God Talks With Arjuna*. Readers who wish to understand the practical application of the Gita's ageless wisdom in the greatest way will want to refer to that larger work.

"The book is a veritable encyclopedia of the spiritual life," wrote the noted yoga scholar Dr. David Frawley. "Yogananda is best known for his *Autobiography of a Yogi*, but his Gita is a work of equal stature and importance. What the *Autobiography* achieves in the realm of human

---

* It should be noted that in the present volume the material appearing in sidebars and footnotes is also taken from Paramahansa Yogananda's words in his comprehensive commentary in *God Talks With Arjuna*, unless otherwise indicated.

experience, *God Talks With Arjuna* achieves as a complete teaching for the spiritual life....

"In his Gita, Yogananda appears as a sage of the highest order and a spiritual scientist, an avatar of yoga for the coming world civilization. The mark of his work will no doubt endure through the ages."

—*Self-Realization Fellowship*

PART I

KEYS
TO THE
GITA'S WISDOM

Bhagavan Krishna and his disciple Arjuna on the battlefield of Kurukshetra.

CHAPTER 1

Introduction to "The Song of the Spirit"

The Bhagavad Gita is the most beloved scripture of India, a scripture of scriptures. It is the Hindu's Holy Testament, or Bible, the one book that all masters depend upon as a supreme source of scriptural authority. *Bhagavad Gita* means "Song of the Spirit," the divine communion of truth-realization between man and his Creator, the teachings of Spirit through the soul, that should be sung unceasingly....

The entire knowledge of the cosmos is packed into the Gita. Supremely profound, yet couched in revelatory language of solacing beauty and simplicity, the Gita has been understood and applied on all levels of human endeavor and spiritual striving—sheltering a vast spectrum of human beings with their disparate natures and needs. Wherever one is on the way back to God, the Gita will shed its light on that segment of the journey.

Wisdom From an Ancient Higher Age of Civilization

India has preserved in her literature her highly evolved civilization dating back to a glorious golden age. From the undated antiquity in which the Vedas first emerged, through a grand unfoldment of subsequent exalted verse and prose, the Hindus have left their civilization not in stone monoliths or crumbling edifices, but in architecture of ornamental writing sculpted in the euphonious language of Sanskrit. The very composition of the Bhagavad Gita—its rhetoric, alliteration, diction, style, and harmony—shows that India had long since passed through states of material and intellectual growth and had arrived at a lofty peak of spirituality.

❖ ❖ ❖

Its verses are found in the sixth of eighteen books that constitute India's great epic poem, the *Mahabharata*....This hoary epic—perhaps the longest poem in world literature—recounts the history of the descendants of King Bharata, the Pandavas and Kauravas, cousins whose dispute over a kingdom was the cause of the cataclysmic war of Kurukshetra. The Bhagavad Gita, a sacred dialogue on yoga between Bhagavan Krishna—who was at once an earthly king and a divine incarnation—and his chief disciple, the Pandava prince Arjuna, purportedly takes place on the eve of this fearsome war.

The authorship of the *Mahabharata*, including the Gita portion, is traditionally assigned to the illumined sage Vyasa, whose date is not definitely known....Tradition involves Vyasa in many literary works, primarily as an arranger of the four Vedas, for which he is referred to as Vedavyasa; compiler of *Puranas*, sacred books illustrating Vedic knowledge through historical and legendary tales of ancient India's avatars, saints and sages, kings and heroes; and author of the epic *Mahabharata*, which purportedly was accomplished nonstop in two and a half of his latter years spent in secluded retirement in the Himalayas.

India's Ageless Wisdom

The testament of the Hindu scriptures is that India's civilization goes back far earlier than contemporary Western historians acknowledge. Swami Sri Yukteswar, in *The Holy Science* (Los Angeles: Self-Realization Fellowship), calculates that the Golden Age, in which India's spiritual and material civilization reached its pinnacle, ended about 6700 B.C. —having flowered for many thousands of years before that. India's scriptural literature lists many generations of kings and sages who lived prior to the events that are the main subject of the *Mahabharata*. In the Gita itself, Krishna describes the long descent of India's spiritual culture from a Golden Age to his own era, as the knowledge of yoga gradually was lost. "Most anthropologists, believing that 10,000 years ago humanity was living in a barbarous Stone Age, summarily dismiss as 'myths' the widespread traditions of very ancient civilizations in Lemuria, Atlantis, India, China, Japan, Egypt, Mexico, and many other lands," a passage in *Autobiography of a Yogi* reads. Recent scientific research, however, is beginning to suggest that the truth of ancient chronologies be reevaluated. *(Publisher's Note)*

Cracking the Code of the Gita's Yogic Symbolism

The ancient sacred writings do not clearly distinguish history from symbology; rather, they often intermix the two in the tradition of scriptural revelation. Prophets would pick up instances of the everyday life and events of their times and from them draw similes to express subtle spiritual truths. Divine profundities would not otherwise be conceivable by the ordinary man unless defined in common terms. When, as they often did, scriptural prophets wrote in more recondite metaphors and allegories, it was to conceal from ignorant, spiritually unprepared minds the deepest revelations of Spirit. Thus, in a language of simile, metaphor, and allegory, the Bhagavad Gita was very cleverly written by Sage Vyasa by interweaving historical facts with psychological and spiritual truths, presenting a word-painting of the tumultuous inner battles that must be waged by both the material and the spiritual man. In the hard shell of symbology, he hid the deepest spiritual meanings to protect them from the devastation of the ignorance of the Dark Ages toward which civilization was descending concurrent with the end of Sri Krishna's incarnation on earth.

Historically, on the brink of such a horrendous war as that related in the *Mahabharata,* it is most unlikely that, as the Gita depicts, Krishna and Arjuna would draw their chariot into the open field between the two opposing armies at Kurukshetra and there engage in an extensive discourse on yoga. While many of the chief events and persons in the compendious *Mahabharata* indeed have their basis in historical fact, their poetic presentation in the epic has been arranged conveniently and meaningfully (and wonderfully condensed in the Bhagavad Gita portion) for the primary purpose of setting forth the essence of India's *Sanatana Dharma,* Eternal Religion.

In interpreting scripture, one must not, therefore, ignore the factual and historical elements in which the truth was couched. One must distinguish between an ordinary illustration of a moral doctrine or recounting of a spiritual phenomenon and that of a deeper esoteric intent. One has to know how to recognize the signs of the convergence of material illustrations with spiritual doctrines without trying to drag a hidden meaning out of everything. One must know how to intuit the cues and express declarations of the author and never fetch out meanings not intended, misled by enthusiasm and the imaginative habit of trying to squeeze spiritual significance from every word or statement.

The true way to understand scripture is through intuition, attuning oneself to the inner realization of truth....Through the help of a God-realized guru, one learns how to use the nutcracker of intuitive perception to crack open the hard shell of language and ambiguity to get at the kernels of truth in scriptural sayings.

My guru, Swami Sri Yukteswar, never permitted me to read with mere theoretical interest any stanza of the Bhagavad Gita (or the aphorisms of Patanjali, India's greatest exponent of Yoga). Master made me meditate on the scriptural truths until I became one with them; then he would discuss them with me....In this way, during those precious years in the blessed company of Master, he gave to me the key to unlock the mystery of scripture.

❖ ❖ ❖

The *Mahabharata* story begins three generations before the time of Krishna and Arjuna, at the time of King Shantanu....

The genealogical descent of the Kurus and Pandus from Shantanu parallels in analogy the step-by-step descent of the universe and man from Spirit into matter. The Gita dialogue concerns itself with the process by which that descent may be reversed, enabling man to reascend from the limited consciousness of himself as a mortal being to the immortal consciousness of his true Self, the soul, one with the infinite Spirit.

The genealogy is diagrammed in [*God Talks With Arjuna*], along with the spiritual significance of the various characters as was handed down from Lahiri Mahasaya. These esoteric meanings are not arbitrary. In explaining the inner meaning of words and names, the primary key is to hunt for it in the original Sanskrit root. Terrible mistakes are made in definitions of Sanskrit terms if there is no intuitive ability to arrive at the correct root, and then to decipher the correct meaning from that root according to its usage at the time of the origin of the word. When the basis is correctly established, one may then also draw meaning from the various sources relative to the common meaning of words and the specific way they were used to form a cogent connective thought.

It is remarkable how the author of this great Bhagavad Gita has clothed every psychological tendency or faculty, as well as many metaphysical principles, with a suitable name. Each word, how beautiful! Each word growing from a Sanskrit root! A proliferation of pages would be required to delve fully into the Sanskrit underlying the metaphors....

It will become evident to the reader after thoughtful perusal of the key to a few stanzas in the first chapter that the historical background of a battle and the contestants therein have been used for the purpose of illustrating the spiritual and psychological battle going on between the attributes of the pure discriminative intellect in attunement with the soul and the blind sense-infatuated mind under the delusive influence of the ego. In support of this analogy, there is shown an exact correspondence between the material and spiritual attributes of man as described by Patanjali in his *Yoga Sutras* and the warring contestants cited in the Gita: the clan of Pandu, representing Pure Intelligence; and that of the blind King Dhritarashtra, representing the Blind Mind with its offspring of wicked sense-tendencies [the Kauravas or Kurus].

These sense bolsheviks—offspring of the blind sense-mind—have brought only sickness, mental worries, and the pestilence of ignorance and spiritual famine, owing to the dearth of wisdom in the bodily kingdom.

The awakened soul force and the meditation-evolved self-control must seize the kingdom and plant therein the banner of Spirit, establishing a reign resplendent with peace, wisdom, abundance, and health.

Bhagavan Krishna, Lord of Yoga: The Divine Teacher of the Gita

The key figure of the Bhagavad Gita is, of course, Bhagavan Krishna. The historical Krishna is enshrouded in the mystery of scriptural metaphor and mythology. Similarities in the titles "Krishna" and "Christ" and in the tales of the miraculous birth and early life of Krishna and Jesus led some analyzing minds to propose that they were indeed one and the same person. This idea can be wholly rejected, based on even scanty historical evidence in the countries of their origin.

Nevertheless, some similarities are there. Both were divinely conceived, and their births and God-ordained missions foretold. Jesus was born in a lowly manger; Krishna, in a prison (where his parents, Vasudeva and Devaki, were held captive by Devaki's wicked brother Kansa, who had usurped the throne of his father). Both Jesus and Krishna were successfully spirited away to safety from a death decree to all male infants meant to seek out and destroy them at birth. Jesus was referred to as the good shepherd; Krishna in his early years was a cowherd. Jesus was tempted and threatened by Satan; the evil force pursued Krishna in demonic forms seeking unsuccessfully to slay him.

"Christ" and "Krishna" are titles having the same spiritual connotation: Jesus the Christ and Yadava the Krishna (Yadava, a family name for Krishna, signifies his descent from Yadu, forerunner of the Vrishni dynasty). These titles identify the state of consciousness manifested by these two illumined beings, their incarnate oneness with the consciousness of God omnipresent in creation. The Universal Christ Consciousness or *Kutastha Chaitanya,* Universal Krishna Consciousness, is "the only begotten son" or sole undistorted reflection of God permeating every atom and point of space in the manifested cosmos. The full measure of God's consciousness is manifested in those who have full realization of the Christ or Krishna Consciousness. As their consciousness is universal, their light is shed on all the world.

A *siddha* is a perfected being who has attained complete liberation in Spirit; he becomes a *paramukta,* "supremely free," and can then return to earth as an *avatara*—as did Krishna, Jesus, and many other saviors of mankind through the ages.* As often as virtue declines, a God-illumined soul comes on earth to draw virtue again to the fore (Gita IV:7–8). An avatar, or divine incarnation, has two purposes on earth: quantitative and qualitative. Quantitatively, he uplifts the general populace with his noble teachings of good against evil. But the main purpose of an avatar is qualitative—to create other God-realized souls, helping as many as possible to attain liberation. This latter is the very personal and private spiritual bond formed between guru and disciple, a union of loyal spiritual endeavor on the part of the disciple and divine blessings bestowed by the guru. Students

---

* The Sanskrit word *avatara* means "descent"; its roots are *ava,* "down," and *tri,* "to pass." In the Hindu scriptures, *avatara* signifies the descent of Divinity into flesh.

are those who receive only a little light of truth. But disciples are those who follow completely and steadfastly, dedicated and devoted, until they have found their own freedom in God. In the Gita, Arjuna stands as the symbol of the ideal devotee, the perfect disciple.

When Sri Krishna incarnated on earth, Arjuna, a great sage in his previous life, took birth also to be his companion. Great ones always bring with them spiritual associates from past lives to assist them in their present mission. Krishna's father was the brother of Arjuna's mother; thus, Krishna and Arjuna were cousins—related by blood, but bound together in an even stronger spiritual unity.

Sri Krishna was raised in a pastoral setting in Gokula and nearby

---

Can God Himself Ever Incarnate as a Human Being?

To say that God can *not* do a certain thing is to limit Him. But there are so many things that God can do, yet does not do—at least not as human beings expect of Him. God has never been known to have taken a human form called "God" and dwelt in it among men. ("Why callest thou me good? There is none good but one, that is, God," Jesus said, to distinguish himself, an avatar, from God the Father, the Absolute, the Formless.) The Lord has condescended many times, however, to manifest Himself through the incarnation of a fully liberated being who, once an ordinary human being, has become a true reflection or "son of God." God, who is almighty and can do anything, thus operates His Omniscience through the human body of an avatar. Just as the ocean of Cosmic Consciousness is aware of a soul wave manifesting on its surface, so the soul wave of an avatar is aware of the ocean of Cosmic Consciousness manifesting through its form.

❖ ❖ ❖

[The foregoing should be kept in mind when reading the many verses in the Gita where Lord Krishna refers to himself as the Supreme Being, such as:]

"For I am the basis of the Infinite, the Immortal, the Indestructible; and of eternal Dharma and unalloyed Bliss." Krishna speaks as the Pratyagatma, the soul or true being of man that is identical with God: Spirit or the Absolute. Krishna's words: "I am the basis of the Infinite," are akin in divine scope to those uttered by Jesus: "Before Abraham was, I am." Krishna and Christ spoke from the depths of Self-realization, knowing that "I and my Father are one."

Brindaban on the banks of the Yamuna River, having been secretly carried there by his father Vasudeva immediately after his birth to Devaki in the prison in Mathura. (Miraculously, the locked doors had opened and the guards had fallen into a deep stupor, allowing the infant to be carried safely to his foster home.) His foster parents were a kindly cowherd Nanda and his loving wife Yasoda. As a child in Brindaban, Krishna amazed all with his precocious wisdom and display of incredible powers. His inner joy frequently erupted in prankish outbursts—to the amusement and delight, and sometimes consternation, of those at whom his fun was directed.

One such incident was the cause of revealing to Yasoda the divine nature of the child she was mothering. The infant Krishna loved to snatch away and consume the cheese made by the milkmaids. Once he had so stuffed his cheeks that Yasoda feared he would choke, so she rushed to pry open his gorged mouth. But instead of cheese (popular accounts say it was mud he had eaten), she beheld in his open mouth the whole universe—the infinite body (*vishvarupa*) of the Creator—including her own image. Awestricken, she turned away from the cosmic vision, happy to see and clasp to her bosom once again her beloved little boy.

Beautiful in form and feature, irresistible in charm and demeanor, an embodiment of divine love, giving joy to all, the young boy Krishna was beloved of everyone in the community, and an entrancing leader and friend to his childhood companions, the *gopas* and *gopis*, who with him tended the village herds of cows in the sylvan environs.

The world, addicted to the senses as the sole means of gratification, can little understand the purity of divine love and friendship that bears no taint of carnal expression or desire. It is absurd to take literally the supposed dalliances of Sri Krishna with the *gopis*. The symbolism is that of the unity of Spirit and Nature, which when dancing together in creation provides a divine *lila*, play, to entertain God's creatures. Sri Krishna, with the enchanting melodies of his heavenly flute, is calling all devotees to the bower of divine union in *samadhi* meditation, there to bask in the blissful love of God.

It would seem that Krishna was hardly more than boy when it came time for him to leave Brindaban in fulfillment of the purpose of his incarnation: to assist the virtuous in restraining evil. His first feat—among many heroic and miraculous exploits—was the destruction of the wicked Kansa and the freeing of his parents Vasudeva and Devaki from prison. Thereafter, he and his brother Balarama were sent by Vasudeva for their education to the ashram of the great sage Sandipani.

Of kingly birth, as an adult Sri Krishna fulfilled his kingly duties, engaging in many campaigns against the reigns of evil rulers. He established the capital of his own kingdom in Dwarka, on an offshore island in the western state of Gujarat. Much of his life is intertwined with that of the Pandavas and the Kauravas, whose capital was in north-central India near the present site of Delhi.* He participated in many of their secular and spiritual affairs as ally and counselor; and was particularly significant in the Kurukshetra war between the Pandus and Kurus. [See sidebar, next page.]

When Sri Krishna had completed his divinely ordained mission on earth, he retired to the forest. There he relinquished his body as a result of an accidental wound inflicted by an arrow from the bow of a hunter who mistook him for a deer as he rested in a glade—an event that had been foretold as the cause of his earth exit.

In the Bhagavad Gita our attention is focused on the role of Sri Krishna as the guru and counselor of Arjuna, and on the sublime yoga message he preached as preceptor to the world—the way of righteous activity and meditation for divine communion and salvation—the wisdom of which has enthroned him in the hearts and minds of devotees throughout the ages.

We hear of saintly ascetics, or prophets in the woods or secluded haunts, who were men of renunciation only; but Sri Krishna was one of the greatest exemplars of divinity, because he lived and manifested himself as a Christ and at the same time performed the duties of a noble king. His life demonstrates the ideal not of renunciation of action—which is a conflicting doctrine for man circumscribed by a world whose life breath is activity—but rather the renunciation of earth-binding desires for the fruits of action.

---

* Kurukshetra, the site of the battlefield and the Gita dialogue between Lord Krishna and Arjuna, is about 100 miles north of Delhi, and is a venerated place of pilgrimage to this day. *(Publisher's Note)*

Krishna's Role in the War of Kurukshetra

The five Pandava princes and the one hundred Kaurava offspring were raised and educated together, receiving the tutelage of their preceptor Drona. Arjuna excelled all of them in prowess; none could match him. Jealousy and enmity grew among the Kauravas against the Pandus....

In time, the dispute between the Kurus and Pandus over the rulership of the kingdom reached a climax. Duryodhana, consumed by jealous desire for supremacy, concocted a cunning scheme: a fraudulent game of dice. Through a clever plot hatched by Duryodhana and his wicked uncle Shakuni, who was an adept in trickery and deceit, Yudhisthira [the eldest Pandava brother] was defeated in throw after throw, finally losing his kingdom, then himself and his brothers, and then their wife Draupadi. Thus Duryodhana filched from the Pandus their kingdom and sent them into exile in the forest for twelve years, and to live a thirteenth year in disguise, unrecognized. Thereafter, if they survived, they could return and lay claim to their lost kingdom. At the allotted time, the good Pandus, having met all the conditions of their exile, returned and demanded their kingdom; but the Kurus refused to part with a piece of land even as long and as broad as a needle.

When war became inevitable, Arjuna for the Pandus and Duryodhana for the Kurus sought Krishna's aid in their cause. Duryodhana arrived first at Krishna's palace and seated himself boldly at the head of the couch upon which Krishna was resting, feigning sleep. Arjuna arrived and stood humbly with folded hands at Krishna's feet. When the avatar opened his eyes, it was, therefore, Arjuna whom he saw first. Both requested Krishna to side with them in the war. Krishna stated that one party could have his massive army, and the other side could have himself as a personal counselor — though he would not take up arms in the combat. Arjuna was given first choice. Without hesitation he wisely chose Krishna himself; the greedy Duryodhana rejoiced to be awarded the army.

Before the war, Krishna served as mediator to try to settle the dispute amicably, journeying from Dwarka to the Kuru capital city at Hastinapura to persuade Dhritarashtra, Duryodhana, and the other Kurus to restore to the Pandavas their rightful kingdom. But even he could not move the power-mad Duryodhana and his followers to accept a fair resolution, and war was declared; the field of conflict was Kurukshetra. The first verse of the Bhagavad Gita begins on the eve of this battle. In the end it was a victory for the Pandus. The five brothers reigned nobly under the kingship of the eldest, Yudhisthira, until at the end of their lives they retired to the Himalayas and there entered the heavenly realm.

Without work human civilization would be a jungle of disease, famine, and confusion. If all the people in the world were to leave their material civilizations and live in the forests, the forests would then have to be transformed into cities, else the inhabitants would die because of lack of sanitation. On the other hand, material civilization is full of imperfections and misery. What possible remedy can be advocated?

Krishna's life demonstrates his philosophy that it is not necessary to flee the responsibilities of material life. The problem can be solved by bringing God here where He has placed us. No matter what our environment may be, into the mind where God-communion reigns, Heaven must come.

A grasping for ever more money, a plunging deeper into more prolonged work with attachment or blindness, will produce misery. Yet mere outward renunciation of material things, if one still harbors an inner attachment to them, leads only to hypocrisy and delusion. To avoid the pitfalls of the two extremes, renunciation of the world, or drowning in material life, man should so train his mind by constant meditation that he can perform the necessary dutiful actions of his daily life and still maintain the consciousness of God within. That is the example set by Krishna's life.

Sri Krishna's message in the Bhagavad Gita is the perfect answer for the modern age, and any age: Yoga of dutiful action, of nonattachment, and of meditation for God-realization. To work without the inner peace of God is Hades; and to work with His joy ever bubbling through the soul is to carry a portable paradise within, wherever one goes.

The path advocated by Sri Krishna in the Bhagavad Gita is the moderate, medium, golden path, both for the busy man of the world and for the highest spiritual aspirant. To follow the path advocated by the Bhagavad Gita would be their salvation, for it is a book of universal Self-realization, introducing man to his true Self, the soul—showing him how he has evolved from Spirit, how he may fulfill on earth his righteous duties, and how he may return to God. The Gita's wisdom is not for dry intellectualists to perform mental gymnastics with its sayings for the entertainment of dogmatists; but rather to show a man or woman living in the world, householder or renunciant, how to live a balanced life that includes the actual contact of God, by following the step-by-step methods of yoga.

CHAPTER 2

The Spiritual Battle of Everyday Life

W e came from God and our ultimate destiny is to return to Him. The end and the means to the end is yoga, the timeless science of God-union.

The opening chapter of the Bhagavad Gita serves as an introduction to the holy discourse that follows. But it does not merely set the scene and provide a backdrop, to be lightly perused as insubstantial. When read as the allegory intended by its author, the great sage Vyasa, it introduces the basic principles of the science of yoga and describes the initial spiritual struggles of the yogi who sets out on the path to *kaivalya*, liberation, oneness with God: the goal of yoga. To understand the implied truths in the first chapter is to begin the yoga journey with a clearly charted course.

Using the Power of Introspection for a Victorious Life

Dhritarashtra said:

"On the holy plain of Kurukshetra (dharmakshetra kurukshetra), when my offspring and the sons of Pandu had gathered together, eager for battle, what did they, O Sanjaya?"

The blind King Dhritarashtra (the blind mind) enquired through the honest Sanjaya (impartial introspection): "When my offspring, the Kurus (the wicked impulsive mental and sense tendencies), and the sons of the virtuous Pandu (the pure discriminative tendencies) gathered together on the *dharmakshetra* (holy plain) of Kurukshetra (the bodily field of activity), eager to do battle for supremacy, what was the outcome?"

Sanjaya means, literally, *completely victorious;* "one who has conquered himself." He alone who is not self-centered has the ability to see clearly and to be impartial. Thus, in the Gita, Sanjaya is divine insight; for the aspiring devotee, Sanjaya represents the power of impartial intuitive self-analysis, discerning introspection. It is the ability to stand aside, observe oneself without any prejudice, and judge accurately. Thoughts may be present without one's conscious awareness. Introspection is that power of intuition by which the consciousness can watch its thoughts. It does not reason, it feels — not with biased emotion, but with clear, calm intuition.

In the *Mahabharata,* of which the Bhagavad Gita is a part, the text of the Gita is introduced by the great *rishi* (sage) Vyasa bestowing on Sanjaya the spiritual power of being able to see from a distance everything taking place over the entire battlefield, so that he could give an account to the blind King Dhritarashtra as the events unfold. Therefore, one would expect the king's enquiry in the first verse to be in the present tense. Author Vyasa purposely had Sanjaya narrate the Gita dialogue retrospectively, and used a past tense of the verb ("What *did* they?"), as a clear hint to discerning students that the Gita is referring only incidentally to a historical battle on the plain of Kurukshetra in northern India. Primarily, Vyasa is describing a universal battle — the one that rages daily in man's life.

The earnest enquiry by the blind King Dhritarashtra, seeking an unbiased report from the impartial Sanjaya as to how fared the battle between the Kurus and the Pandavas (sons of Pandu) at Kurukshetra, is metaphorically the question to be asked by the spiritual aspirant as he reviews daily the events of his own righteous battle from which he seeks the victory of Self-realization. Through honest introspection he analyzes the deeds and assesses the strengths of the opposing armies of his good and bad tendencies: self-control versus sense indulgence, discriminative intelligence opposed by mental sense inclinations, spiritual resolve in meditation contested by mental resistance and physical restlessness, and divine soul-consciousness against the ignorance and magnetic attraction of the lower ego-nature.

The Spiritual Battlefield of Man's Body and Mind

The battlefield of these contending forces is Kurukshetra (*Kuru,* from the Sanskrit root *kri,* "work, material action"; and *kṣetra,* "field"). This "field of action" is the human body with its physical, mental, and soul faculties, the field on which all activities of one's life take place. It is referred to in this Gita stanza as Dharmakshetra (*dharma,* i.e., righteousness, virtue, holiness; thus, holy plain or field), for on this field the righteous battle is waged between the virtues of the soul's discriminative intelligence (sons of Pandu) and the ignoble, uncontrolled activities of the blind mind (the Kurus, or offspring of the blind King Dhritarashtra).

Dharmakshetra Kurukshetra refers also, respectively, to religious and spiritual duties and activities (those of the yogi in meditation) as contrasted with mundane responsibilities and activities. Thus, in this deeper metaphysical interpretation, Dharmakshetra Kurukshetra signifies the inner bodily field on which the spiritual action of yoga meditation takes place for the attainment of Self-realization: the plain of the cerebrospinal axis and its seven subtle centers of life and divine consciousness. [See sidebar, "The Chakras in the Cerebrospinal Axis," page 21.]

Material Consciousness Versus Spiritual Consciousness

Competing on this field are two opposing forces or magnetic poles: discriminative intelligence (*buddhi*) and the sense-conscious mind (*manas*).

Buddhi, the pure discriminating intellect, is allegorically represented as Pandu, husband of Kunti (the mother of Arjuna and the other Pandava princes who uphold the righteous principles of *nivritti,* renunciation of worldliness). The name Pandu derives from *pand,* "white"—a metaphorical implication of the clarity of a pure discriminating intellect.

Manas is allegorically represented as the blind King Dhritarashtra, sire of the one hundred Kurus, or sensory impressions and inclinations, which are all bent toward *pravritti,* worldly enjoyment.

Buddhi draws its right discernment from the superconsciousness of the soul manifesting in the causal seats of consciousness in the spiritual cerebrospinal centers. *Manas,* the sense mind, the subtle magnetic pole turned outward toward the world of matter, is in the pons Varolii, which physiologically is ever busy with sensory coordination.*

Thus, *buddhi* intelligence draws the consciousness toward truth or the eternal realities, soul consciousness or Self-realization. *Manas* or sense mind repels the consciousness from truth and engages it in the external sensory activities of the body, and thus with the world of delusive relativities, *maya.*

The name Dhritarashtra derives from *dhṛta,* "held, supported, drawn tight (reins)," and *raṣṭra,* "kingdom," from *rāj,* "to rule." By implication, we have the symbolic meaning, *dhṛtam raṣṭram yena,* "who upholds the kingdom (of the senses)," or "who rules by holding tightly the reins (of the senses)."

The mind (*manas,* or sense consciousness) gives coordination to the senses as the reins keep together the several horses of a chariot. The body is the chariot; the soul is the owner of the chariot; intelligence is the charioteer; the senses are the horses. The mind is said to be blind because it cannot see without the help of the senses and intelligence. The reins of a chariot receive and relay the impulses from the steeds and the guidance of the charioteer. Similarly, the blind mind on its own neither cognizes nor exerts guidance, but merely receives the impressions from the senses and relays the conclusions and instructions of the intelligence.

If the intelligence is governed by *buddhi,* the pure discriminative power, the senses are controlled; if the intelligence is ruled by material desires, the senses are wild and unruly....They fall into evil ways and self-destructive habits.

A devotee moving toward Self-realization should have a healthy

---

* The pons Varolii is a part of the brain stem—situated above the medulla and centered below the two hemispheres of the cerebrum—connecting the cerebrum, cerebellum, and medulla. Small in size (1 x 1 x 1 ½ inches), it contains the ascending sensory and descending motor tracts that connect the brain to the rest of the body. These tracts travel through a dense network of nerve cells, called the reticular formation, whose function is to arouse to activity the rest of the brain and to regulate the twenty-four-hour cycle of sleep and waking. The pons Varolii contains a particular structure, the locus coeruleus ("blue place")—a small, concentrated cluster of cells containing norepinephrine, a chemical substance that stimulates the mobilization that prepares the body for action. This structure is involved in arousal, dreaming, sleep, and mood.

body, well-behaved senses trained by self-control, strong mental reins to hold them, and a keen discriminative intelligence to guide them. Then the body-chariot can traverse the straight and narrow path of right action to its destination....

A worldly man in a vulnerable body, who has poor discrimination and weak mental faculties, and who thus allows his strong impulses to roam at will, uncontrolled, over the rough road of life, will surely meet with a disastrous fate of wrecked health and material failures....

The devotee is aware that the most important objective in life is to attain the goal of Self-realization: to know through meditation his true soul nature and its oneness with ever blissful Spirit. That he may not be waylaid by tumbling into ditches of physical, mental, and spiritual suffering, he learns also to develop discriminative intelligence, clear harmonious mental faculties of perception, self-controlled senses, and a body imbued with health and vitality—that they may all serve the soul.

Taking Sides in the War of Good Against Evil

From the moment of conception to the surrender of the last breath, man has to fight in each incarnation innumerable battles—biological, hereditary, bacteriological, physiological, climatic, social, ethical, political, sociological, psychological, metaphysical—so many varieties of inner and outer conflicts. Competing for victory in every encounter are the forces of good and evil.* The whole intent of the Gita is to align man's efforts on the side of *dharma,* or righteousness. The ultimate aim is Self-realization, the realization of man's true Self, the soul, as made in the image of God, one with the ever-existing, ever-conscious, ever-new bliss of Spirit.

The first contest of the soul in each incarnation is with other souls seeking rebirth. With the union of sperm and ovum to begin the formation of a new human body, a flash of light appears in the astral world, the heavenly home of souls between incarnations. That light transmits a pattern which attracts a soul according to that soul's karma—the self-

---

* "Good" being that which expresses truth and virtue and attracts the consciousness to God; and "evil" being ignorance and delusion, that which repels the consciousness from God.

created influences from actions of past lives. In each incarnation, karma works itself out partly through hereditary forces; the soul of a child is attracted into a family in which heredity is in conformance with the child's past karma. Many souls vie to enter this new cell of life; only one will be victorious. (In the case of a multiple conception, more than one primal cell is present.)

Within the mother's body, the unborn child struggles against disease, darkness, and periodic feelings of limitation and frustration as the soul consciousness in the unborn child remembers and then gradually forgets its greater freedom of expression during its astral sojourn. The soul within the embryo also has to contend with karma, which is influencing for good or ill the formation of the body in which it is now a resident. Additionally, it encounters the vibratory influences that reach it from outside—the environment and actions of the mother; external sounds and sensations; vibrations of love and hate, peace and anger.

After birth, the struggles of the infant are between its instincts to seek comfort and survival and the opposing relative helplessness of its immature bodily instrument.

A child begins his first conscious struggle when he has to choose between his desires to play aimlessly and his desire to learn, study, and pursue some course of systematic training. Gradually, more serious battles arise, forced upon him by karmic instincts from within or by bad company and environment from without.

The youth finds himself confronted suddenly with a host of problems that often he has been ill-prepared to meet: temptations of sex, greed, prevarication, money-making by easy but questionable means, pressure from the company he keeps, and social influences. The youth usually discovers he possesses no sword of wisdom with which to fight the invading armies of worldly experiences.

The adult who lives without cultivating and employing his innate powers of wisdom and spiritual discrimination finds inexorably that the kingdom of his body and mind is being overrun by the insurgents of misery-making wrong desires, destructive habits, failure, ignorance, disease, and unhappiness.

Few men are even aware that a state of constant warfare exists in their kingdom. Usually, it is only when the devastation is nearly complete that men helplessly realize the sad ruin of their lives. The psychological conflict for health, prosperity, self-control, and wisdom has to be started anew each day in order for man to advance toward victory, reclaiming inch by inch the territories of the soul occupied by the rebels of ignorance.

The yogi, the awakening man, is confronted not only with the external battles fought by all men, but also with the internal clash between the negative forces of restlessness (arising from *manas,* or sense consciousness) and the positive power of his desire and effort to meditate (supported by *buddhi* intelligence) when he tries to reestablish himself in the soul's inner spiritual kingdom: the subtle centers of life and divine consciousness in the spine and brain.

The Gita therefore points out in its very first stanza the prime necessity to man of nightly introspection, that he may clearly discern which force—the good or the evil—has won the daily battle. To live in harmony with God's plan, man must ask himself each night the ever pertinent question: "Gathered together on the sacred bodily tract—the field of good and evil actions—what did my opposing tendencies do? Which side won today in the ceaseless struggle? The crooked, tempting, evil tendencies, and the opposing forces of self-discipline and discrimination—come now, tell me, what did they do?"

The yogi, after each practice of concentrated meditation, asks his power of introspection: "Assembled in the region of consciousness in the cerebrospinal axis and on the field of the body's sensory activity, eager for battle, the mental sense-faculties that try to pull the consciousness outward, and the children of the soul's discriminative tendencies that seek to reclaim the inner kingdom—what did they? who won this day?"

The ordinary individual, like a skirmish-scarred beleaguered warrior, is all too conversant with the battles. But often his haphazard training has been wanting in an understanding of the battlefield, and of the science behind the attacks of the opposing forces. That knowledge would increase his victories, and lessen the bewildering defeats.

The Chakras in the Cerebrospinal Axis

Yoga treatises identify these seven centers (in ascending order) as: 1) *muladhara* (the coccygeal, at the base of the spine); 2) *svadhisthana* (the sacral, two inches above *muladhara*); 3) *manipura* (the lumbar, opposite the navel); 4) *anahata* (the dorsal, opposite the heart); 5) *vishuddha* (the cervical, at the base of the neck); 6) *ajna* (seat of the spiritual eye, traditionally located between the eyebrows; in actuality, directly connected by polarity with the medulla oblongata); 7) *sahasrara* ("thousand-petaled lotus" at the top of the cerebrum).

The seven centers are divinely planned exits or "trap doors" through which the soul has descended into the body and through which it must reascend by a process of meditation.

The life current flowing downward from the brain carries the mind to the senses and to identity with the physical body and the domain of entangling matter. By a technique such as *Kriya Yoga,* the life current is reversed to flow upward to the centers of spiritual perception in the brain, carrying the mind from the senses to the soul and Spirit....

When the yogi withdraws the life force from material objects, sensory organs, and sensory-motor nerves and takes the concentrated life upward through the spiral passageway of *kundalini* (coiled energy) in the coccyx, he perceives, as he ascends, the various spinal centers with their petaled light-rays and sounds of life energy. When the yogi's consciousness reaches the medulla and the spiritual eye at the point between the eyebrows, he finds the doorway into the star-lotus of "a thousand" (innumerable) rays. He perceives the omnipresent light of God spreading over the sphere of eternity, and his body as a minuscule emanation of this light.

❖ ❖ ❖

All of the astral cerebrospinal plexuses in their natural state are spiritual, reflecting the diverse aspects of the divine intelligence and vibratory power of the superconsciousness of the soul. But when the energies of these centers are drawn outward under the influence of the senses, and their connection with the soul's pure discriminatory faculty is diminished, their expression becomes proportionately perverted. The externalized cerebral centers express intellect, reason, and distorting restlessness (rather than the all-knowing wisdom of intuition and Spirit-reflecting calmness). The externalized heart center, when identified with the senses, expresses itself as the activating impulses of emotional likes and dislikes, attachments and aversions (rather than pure unprejudiced feeling and life-force control). The externalized three lower centers feed the avaricious appetites of the senses (rather than expressing the divine potentials of these *chakras:* self-control, adherence to virtuous principles, and the power of resisting wrong influences).

Soul Versus Ego

In the historical telling of the cause of the war of Kurukshetra, the noble sons of Pandu reigned virtuously over their kingdom, until King Duryodhana, the wicked reigning son of the blind King Dhritarashtra, cleverly took away from the Pandavas their kingdom, and banished them into exile.*

Symbolically, the kingdom of body and mind rightfully belongs to King Soul and his noble subjects of virtuous tendencies. But King Ego and his kinsmen of wicked, ignoble tendencies cunningly usurp the throne. When King Soul arises to reclaim his territory, the body and mind become the battleground.†

How King Soul rules over his bodily kingdom, loses and then regains it, is the essence of the Gita.

The organization of man's body and mind reveals, in its detailed perfection, the presence of a divine plan. "Know ye not that ye are the temple of God, and that the Spirit of God dwelleth in you?"‡ The Spirit of God, His reflection in man, is the soul.

The soul makes its entry into matter as a spark of omnipotent life and consciousness within the nucleus formed by the union of the sperm and ovum. As the body develops, this original "seat of life" remains in the medulla oblongata. The medulla is therefore referred to as the gateway of life through which King Soul makes his triumphal entrance into the bodily kingdom....

The creative faculties or instruments of the soul are astral and causal

---

* The blind King Dhritarashtra had one hundred sons....The eldest, Duryodhana, represents Material Desire—the firstborn, that which wields power over all the other sense inclinations of the bodily kingdom. He is one who is well-known for evil wars or causes. The metaphorical derivation of Duryodhana is *duḥ-yudhaṁ yaḥ saḥ*—"one who is hard to be countered in any way." His very name comes from the Sanskrit *dur,* "difficult" and *yudh,* "to fight." Material desire is extremely powerful, for it is the king and leader of all worldly enjoyments, and is the cause and perpetrator of the battle against the soul's rightful claim to the bodily kingdom.

†Here the epithets King Soul and King Ego are used in the broader sense of their meaning, and not necessarily referring to their specific usage in the Gita allegory wherein Krishna is the soul and Bhishma, the ego.

‡I Corinthians 3:16.

in nature....The centers of life and consciousness from which these powers function are the astral brain (or "thousand-petaled lotus" of light), and the astral cerebrospinal axis (or *sushumna*) containing six subtle centers or *chakras*.*

Coarser forces of the mind manifest in grosser structures of the body, but the fine forces of the soul—consciousness, intelligence, will, feeling—require the medulla and delicate tissues of the brain in which to dwell and through which to manifest.

In simplistic terms, the inner chambers of the palace of King Soul are in the subtle centers of superconsciousness, Christ or Krishna Consciousness (*Kutastha Chaitanya,* or Universal Consciousness), and Cosmic Consciousness. These centers are, respectively, in the medulla, frontal part of the brain between the eyebrows (seat of the single or spiritual eye), and at the top of the cerebrum (the throne of the soul, in the "thousand-petaled lotus"). In these states of consciousness, King Soul reigns supreme—the pure image of God in man.

But when the soul descends into body consciousness, it comes under the influence of *maya* (cosmic delusion) and *avidya* (individual delusion or ignorance, which creates ego consciousness)....The soul, as the ego, ascribes to itself all the limitations and circumscriptions of the body. Once so identified, the soul can no longer express its omnipresence, omniscience, and omnipotence. It imagines itself to be limited—just as a rich prince, wandering in a state of amnesia in the slums, might imagine himself to be a pauper. In this state of delusion, King Ego takes command of the bodily kingdom.

The soul consciousness can say with the awakened Christ in Jesus, "I and my Father are one." The deluded ego consciousness says, "I am the body; this is my family and name; these are my possessions." Though

---

* In human life the soul is encased in three bodies: the physical body, the astral body of light and life-energy, and the causal body of consciousness (so named because it is the cause of the other two bodies). The subtle powers in the astral body are what build, maintain, and enliven the gross physical form; these powers consist of: intelligence (*buddhi*); ego (*ahamkara*); feeling (*chitta*); mind (*manas,* sense consciousness); five instruments of knowledge; five instruments of action; and five instruments of *prana*.

ego thinks it rules, it is in reality a prisoner of the body and mind, which in turn are pawns of the subtle machinations of Cosmic Nature....The average human being is conscious only of his body and mind and of their outer connections. He remains hypnotized by the world delusions (expressed in many ways in ancient and present-day literature) which reinforce his tacit assumption that he is a finite and limited creature.

The physical tracts of the bodily kingdom under King Ego are often fallow and unhealthy from epidemics of diseases and premature aging that spread over the realm....The citizenry of thoughts, will, feelings, become negative, limited, jaded, unhappy; the intelligent workers of cells and atomic and subatomic units of life become disorganized, inefficient, debilitated....All laws are broken that would lead to the well-being of the mental and cellular citizens in man's kingdom. It is a realm of darkness fraught with many fears, uncertainties, and miseries to counteract every brief moment of pleasure.

[In] the bodily kingdom under the rule of King Soul....the citizenry of thoughts, will, and feelings are wise, constructive, peaceful, and happy. The masses of conscious, intelligent laborers of cells, molecules, atoms, electrons, and units of creative life sparks (lifetrons, *prana*) are vital, harmonious, efficient....All laws regarding the health, the mental efficiency, and the spiritual education of the thoughts, will, feelings, and intelligent cellular inhabitants of the bodily kingdom are carried on under the supreme guidance of wisdom. As a result, happiness, health, prosperity, peace, discrimination, efficiency, and intuitive guidance pervade the bodily kingdom—a pure realm of light and bliss!

The human body and mind are veritable battlegrounds for the war between wisdom and the conscious delusive force manifesting as *avidya,* ignorance. Every spiritual aspirant, aiming to establish within himself the rule of King Soul, must defeat the rebels, King Ego and his powerful allies.

Yoga: The Method of Victory

The practical metaphysician, in the course of his attempts to free his soul from material bondage, learns the exact methods for victory.

By consistently right thoughts and actions, in harmony with divine law, the soul of man ascends slowly in the course of natural evolution. The yogi, however, chooses the quicker evolution-hastening method: scientific meditation, by which the flow of consciousness is reversed from matter to Spirit through the same cerebrospinal centers of life and divine consciousness that channeled the soul's descent into the body.

Behind the energetic forces in each center is an expression of the divine consciousness of the soul....Through each triumphant contact with Spirit [in meditation], the soul consciousness becomes strengthened and more firmly in control of the bodily kingdom.

Even the novitiate meditator quickly finds that he is able to draw upon the spiritual power and consciousness of the inner world of soul and Spirit to enlighten his bodily kingdom and activities—physical, mental, and spiritual. The more adept he becomes, the greater the divine influence.

Activating the Soul's Powers Through Meditation

The pure discriminative powers [are] symbolically represented as the five divine sons of Pandu....The five Pandavas are the central heroic figures of the Gita analogy, controlling the armies of consciousness and energy (*prana*) in the five subtle centers of the spine. They represent the qualities and powers acquired by the devotee whose deep meditation is attuned to the astral and causal centers of life and divine consciousness.

In ascending order, the significance of the five Pandavas is as follows:

Sahadeva: Restraint, Power to Stay Away From Evil (*Dama,* the active power of resistance, tenacity, by which restless outer sense organs can be controlled); and the vibratory earth element in the coccyx center, or *muladhara chakra.**

Nakula: Adherence, Power to Obey Good Rules (*Sama,* the positive or absorbing power, attention, by which mental tendencies can be controlled); and the vibrating water element in the sacral center, or *svadhishthana chakra.*

Arjuna: Self-Control; and the vibratory fire element in the lumbar center. This center, the *manipura chakra,* bestows the fire-force of mental and bodily strength to fight against the vast onslaught of the sense soldiers. It is the reinforcer of good habits and actions; the habit trainer. It holds the body upright, and causes purification of the body and mind, and makes deep meditation possible.

We see further why this center allegorically represents Arjuna, the most skilled of all the Pandava army, when we consider its dual function. It is the pivotal or turning point of the devotee's life from gross materialism to finer spiritual qualities. From the lumbar to the sacral and coccygeal centers life and consciousness flow downward and outward to materialistic, sense-bound body consciousness. But in meditation, when the devotee assists the life and consciousness to be attracted to the magnetic pull in the higher or dorsal center, the power of this fiery lumbar center dissociates itself from material concerns and upholds the spiritual work of the devotee through the powers in the higher centers....

When Arjuna, the power of self-control in the lumbar center, rouses the fire of meditation and spiritual patience and determination, he draws upward the life and consciousness that was flowing downward and outward through the lumbar, sacral, and coccygeal centers, and thereby

* The vibratory elements (*tattvas*) in each *chakra* are subtle forces by which the different forms of matter are manifested from the creative Light of Spirit. They are explained in *God Talks With Arjuna. (Publisher's Note)*

gives the meditating yogi the necessary mental and bodily strength to pursue the course of deep meditation leading to Self-realization. Without this fire and self-control, no spiritual progress is possible. Thus Arjuna, more literally, also represents the devotee of self-control, patience, and determination within whom the battle of Kurukshetra is taking place. He is the chief devotee and disciple of the Lord, Bhagavan Krishna, who in the Gita dialogue is being shown by Krishna the way to victory.

The remaining two Pandavas are:

Bhima: Power of Vitality, soul-controlled life force (*prana*); and the vibratory creative air (or *prana*) element in the dorsal center, or *anahata chakra*. The power of this center aids the devotee in the practice of the right techniques of *pranayama* to calm the breath and control the mind and sensory onslaughts. It is the power to still the internal and external organs and thus destroy the invasion of any passion (as of sex, greed, or anger). It is the destroyer of disease and doubt. It is the center of divine love and spiritual creativity. [See sidebar, page 44.]

Yudhisthira: Divine Calmness; and the creative vibratory ether element in the cervical center, or *vishuddha chakra*. Yudhisthira, the eldest of the five offspring of Pandu (*buddhi*, or pure intellect) is fittingly portrayed as the king of all discriminative faculties, for calmness is the principal factor necessary for any expression of right discernment.

Anything that ripples the consciousness, sensual or emotional, distorts whatever is perceived. But calmness is clarity of perception, intuition itself. As the ubiquitous ether remains unchanged, notwithstanding the violent roil of Nature's forces that play upon it, so the Yudhisthira discriminative faculty is the immutable calmness that discerns all things without distortion.

It is the power of being able to plan the overthrow of an enemy passion. It is the power of attention, continued attention on the right object. It governs the span of attention, and the penetration of attention.

It is the power of inference of the effects of wrong actions, and the power of assimilation of goodness through calmness.

It is the power of comparison between good and evil; and common sense in perceiving the virtue of reinforcing a friend and destroying an enemy (as of the senses and habits, for example).

It is the power of intuitive imagination, the ability to image or visualize a truth until it manifests.

The Pandavas' chief counsellor and support is the Lord Himself, who, in the form of Krishna, represents variously the Spirit, the soul, or intuition as manifested in the states of superconsciousness, *Kutastha* or Christ consciousness, and cosmic consciousness in the medulla, Christ center, and thousand-petaled lotus; or as the guru instructing his disciple, the devotee Arjuna. Within the devotee, Lord Krishna is thus the guiding Divine Intelligence speaking to the lower self that has gone astray in the entanglements of sensory consciousness. This Higher Intelligence is the master and teacher, and the lower mental intellect is the disciple; the Higher Intelligence advises the lower vitiated self on how to uplift itself in accord with the eternal verities, and in fulfillment of its inherent God-given duty.

Spiritual Effects of the Practice of Yoga

A popular misconception is that the practice of yoga is for adept mystics only, and that this science is beyond even the ken of ordinary man. Yet yoga is the science of the whole creation. Man, as also every atom in the universe, is an externalized result of this divine science at work. The practice of yoga is a set of disciplines through which an understanding of this science unfolds through direct personal experience of God, the Supreme Cause.

The material scientist starts with the observable effect of matter and attempts to work backward toward a cause. Yoga, on the other hand, describes the Cause and how it evolved outward into the phenomena of matter, and shows how to follow that process in *reverse* to experience the true Spirit-nature of the universe and man....

India's great sage Patanjali, whose date is a matter of conjecture by the scholars, understood that the Bhagavad Gita was the "Song Celestial" by which the Lord wanted to unite the soul of His ignorant and wandering children with His own Spirit. This was to be accomplished scientifically through physical, mental, and spiritual law. Patanjali explained this spiritual science in definite metaphysical terms in his renowned *Yoga Sutras*....

The intent of the Gita is brought immediately into focus when we see how each of the warriors mentioned in verses 4 through 8 relate to the practice of yoga as described by Patanjali in his *Yoga Sutras*. The correlation is found in the metaphorical significance of the various metaphysical warriors, implied in the meaning derived from their names, or from a Sanskrit root within their names, or from their significance in the *Mahabharata* epic.

In verses 4, 5, and 6, King Desire (Duryodhana) informs his preceptor Past Habit (Drona) about the spiritual soldiers in the cerebrospinal centers that have lined up in battle array. These metaphysical soldiers, which have gathered to support the cause of the five Pandavas, are the spiritual effects engendered by the devotee's practice of yoga. They, along with the five principal Pandavas, come to the aid of the yogi to help him battle the evil soldiers of the sense mind.

Duryodhana identifies them as Yuyudhana, Virata, Drupada, Dhrishtaketu, Chekitana, King of Kashi (Kashiraja), Purujit, Kuntibhoja, Shaibya, Yudhamanyu, Uttamaujas, the son of Subhadra (Abhimanyu), and the five sons of Draupadi. Their metaphorical significance will be explained in the categorical order adopted by Patanjali.

Patanjali begins his *Yoga Sutras* with the definition of yoga as "the neutralization of the alternating waves in consciousness" (*chitta vritti nirodha*—I:2). This may also be translated as "cessation of the modifications of the mind-stuff."

I have explained in *Autobiography of a Yogi*, "*Chitta* is a comprehensive term for the thinking principle, which includes the pranic life forces, *manas* (mind or sense consciousness), *ahamkara* (egoity), and *buddhi* (intuitive intelligence). *Vritti* (literally 'whirlpool') refers to the waves of thought and emotion that ceaselessly arise and subside in man's consciousness. *Nirodha* means neutralization, cessation, control."

Patanjali continues: "Then the seer abides in his own nature or self" (I:3). This refers to his true Self, or soul. That is, he attains Self-realization, oneness of his soul with God.

Patanjali explains in *sutras* I:20–21: "[The attainment of this goal of yoga] is preceded by *shraddha* (devotion), *virya* (vital celibacy), *smriti* (memory), *samadhi* (the experience of God-union during meditation), *prajna* (discriminative intelligence). Its attainment is nearest to those possessing *tivra-samvega*, divine ardor (fervent devotion and striving for God, and extreme dispassion toward the world of the senses)."

From these *sutras* we have the first six metaphysical soldiers, which stand in readiness to aid the yogi's battle for Self-realization:

1. Yuyudhana—Divine Devotion (Shraddha)

From the Sanskrit root *yudh*, "to fight," Yuyudhana means literally "he who has been fighting for his own benefit." The metaphorical derivation: *Yudham caitanya-prakāśayitum eṣanaḥ abhilaṣamāna iti*—"One who has an ardent desire to fight to express spiritual consciousness." It represents the attracting principle of love whose "duty" it is to draw creation back to God. Felt by the devotee as *shraddha*, or devotion for God, it is an inherent pull of the heart in longing to know Him. It stirs the devotee to spiritual action and supports his *sadhana* (spiritual practices).

Shraddha is frequently translated as faith; but it is more accurately defined as the natural inclination, or devotion, of the heart quality to turn toward its Source, and faith is an integral part of surrendering to this pull. Creation is a result of repulsion, a going away from God—an externalization of Spirit. But inherent in matter is the force of attraction. This is the love of God, a magnet that ultimately pulls creation back to Him. The more the devotee is attuned to it, the stronger the pull becomes, and the sweeter the purifying effects of the yogi's divine devotion.

Yuyudhana, Divine Devotion, fights the forces of irreverent satanic disbelief or doubt, which try to dissuade and discourage the aspirant.

2. Uttamaujas—Vital Celibacy (Virya)

The literal meaning of Uttamaujas, the *Mahabharata* warrior, is "of excellent valor." The common interpretation given to Patanjali's *virya* is heroism or courage. But in yoga philosophy, *virya* also refers to the creative semen, which, if instead of being sensually dissipated is transmuted into its pure vital essence, gives great bodily strength, vitality, and moral courage. Thus we find that Uttamaujas from the Sanskrit *uttama*, "chief, principal" and *ojas,* "energy, power, bodily strength," may also be translated as "the principal power, the chief bodily strength." Thus, the metaphorical derivation: *Uttamam oja yasya sa iti*—"One whose power is supreme (of highest or superlative quality)." The vital essence, when mastered by the yogi, is a principal source of his spiritual strength and moral fortitude.*

The vital essence, the sense mind, the breath, and *prana* (the life force or vitality) are closely interrelated. Mastery of even one gives control over the other three also. The devotee who employs scientific yoga techniques to control simultaneously all four forces quickly reaches a higher state of consciousness.

Uttamaujas, Vital Celibacy, lends its power to the devotee to defeat the forces of temptations and habits of debauchery, and thus to free the life force to be lifted up from gross pleasure to divine bliss.

3. Chekitana—Spiritual Memory (Smriti)

Chekitana means "intelligent." From its Sanskrit root *chit* come the derivative meanings, "to appear, to shine, to remember." The metaphorical derivation: *Ciketi jānāti iti*—"He remembers, realizes, true knowledge whose perception is clear, concentrated." Patanjali's *smriti* means memory, divine and human. It is that faculty by which the yogi recalls his true nature as made in the image of God. As this memory appears or shines on his consciousness, it gives him that intelligence or clear perception which helps to light his path.

Chekitana, Spiritual Memory, stands in readiness to oppose the material delusion that makes man forget God and consider himself a body-bound mortal being.

---

* In his commentary in *God Talks With Arjuna,* Paramahansa Yogananda elaborated in detail on the Gita's teaching regarding right use and control of the sexual impulse. An excerpt: "The beginner in yoga meditation experiences all too definitely how grounded he is by the stubborn attachment of his life and energy to the body, sometimes without realizing that it is his uncontrolled thoughts and acts of sex that are primarily responsible for his earthbound condition. The seeker after Self-realization is therefore urged by yoga to take command of this rebel force: married couples should practice moderation, with love and friendship predominating; the unmarried should abide by the pure laws of celibacy—in thought as well as in act....Because suppression may only increase one's difficulties, yoga teaches sublimation....The insatiable desire for the pleasure of sex is transmuted by the divine love and ecstatic joy experienced in deep meditation."

4. Virata — Ecstasy (Samadhi)

When the five Pandavas were exiled from their kingdom by Dur-yodhana, the conditions were that they must spend twelve years in the forest and that in the thirteenth year they must live undiscovered by the spies of Duryodhana. Thus it was that the Pandavas spent the thirteenth year in disguise in the court of King Virata.

The metaphorical significance is that once material desires as habits take complete control, it requires a cycle of twelve years to rid the bodily kingdom of the usurpers. Before the rightful discriminative qualities can regain their kingdom, the devotee must draw those qualities from his experiences in *samadhi* meditation, and then be able to hold on to them while expressing through the physical body and senses. When the discriminative qualities have thus proven their power, they are ready for the metaphysical battle to reclaim their bodily kingdom.

Thus, Virata represents Patanjali's *samadhi,* the temporary states of divine union in meditation from which the yogi draws spiritual strength. Virata comes from the Sanskrit *vi-rāj,* "to rule, to shine forth." *Vi* expresses distinction, opposition, implying the difference between ruling in an ordinary way and ruling or reigning from the divine consciousness experienced in *samadhi.* The metaphorical derivation: *Viśeṣeṇa ātmani rājate iti* — "One who is wholly immersed in his inner Self." Under the influence or rule of *samadhi,* the devotee himself is illuminated and governs his actions by divine wisdom.

Virata, Samadhi, the state of oneness with God attained during deep meditation, routs the delusion that has made the soul behold, through its ego nature, not the One True Spirit, but the diverse forms of matter and the pairs of opposites.

5. Kashiraja — Discriminative Intelligence (Prajna)

The word Kashiraja derives from *kāśi,* "shining, splendid, brilliant," and *rāj,* "to reign, to rule, to shine." It means to reign with light, or in a splendid or brilliant way; the light that reveals the substance behind the seeming. The metaphorical derivation: *Padārthān kāśyan prakāśayan rājate vibhāti iti* — "One whose shining causes other things to shine (to be accurately revealed)." This ally of the Pandavas represents Patanjali's *prajna,* discriminative intelligence—insight or wisdom—which is the principal enlightening faculty in the devotee. *Prajna* is not the mere intellect of the scholar, bound by logic, reason, and memory, but an expression of the divine faculty of the Supreme Knower.

Kashiraja, Discriminative Intelligence, protects the devotee from entrapment by the cunning troops of false reasoning.

6. Drupada—Extreme Dispassion (Tivra-samvega)

The literal translation of the Sanskrit roots in Drupada are *dru,* "to run, hasten," and *pada,* "pace or step." The metaphorical derivation: *Drutam padam yasya sa iti*—"One whose steps are quick, or swift." The implied meaning is one who advances swiftly. This correlates with Patanjali's *tivra-samvega;* literally, *tīvra,* "extreme," and *samvega,* from *sam,* "together," and *vij,* "to move quickly, to speed."

The word *samvega* also means dispassion toward the things of the world arising from an ardent longing for emancipation. This dispassionate detachment from worldly objects and concerns is referred to elsewhere in the Gita as *vairagya.* Patanjali says, as cited earlier, that the goal of yoga is nearest (that is, is reached most quickly by) those who possess *tivra-samvega.* This intense dispassion is not a negative disinterest or deprived state of renunciation. The meaning of the word rather encompasses such an ardent devotion for attaining the spiritual goal—a feeling that stirs the devotee into positive action and mental intensity—that longing for the world is transmuted naturally into a fulfilling desire for God.

Drupada, Extreme Dispassion, supports the devotee's fight against the strong army of material attachment that seeks to turn him from his spiritual goal.

Awakening the Eightfold Essence of Yoga Within Yourself

The next Pandava allies represent the essentials of yoga. These *yog-angas,* or limbs of yoga, have come to be known as Patanjali's Eightfold Path of Yoga. They are enumerated in his *Yoga Sutras,* II:29: *Yama* (moral conduct, the avoidance of immoral actions); *niyama* (religious observances); *asana* (right posture for bodily and mental control); *pranayama* (control of *prana* or life force); *pratyahara* (interiorization of the mind); *dhar-*

ana (concentration); *dhyana* (meditation); and *samadhi* (divine union).

Continuing, then, to describe the metaphysical soldiers:

7. Dhrishtaketu—Power of Mental Resistance (Yama)

In the Sanskrit root *dhriṣ* are the meanings, "to be bold and courageous; to dare to attack." *Ketu* means "chief or leader"; also "brightness, clearness; intellect, judgment." The metaphorical derivation: *Yana ketavaḥ āpadaḥ dhṛṣyate anena iti*—"One by whose discriminative intellect difficulties are overpowered." The object against which Dhrishtaketu directs his power is found also within his name. In addition to meaning bold and daring, *dhrishta* means "licentious." Dhrishtaketu represents that power within the devotee which has the right judgment to attack with courage—that is, the mental power to resist—evil inclinations toward immoral behavior. It thus represents Patanjali's *yama*, moral conduct. This first step of the Eightfold Path is fulfilled by observing the "thou shalt nots"—abstaining from injury to others, falsehood, stealing, incontinence, and covetousness. Understood in the full sense of their meaning, these proscripts embrace the whole of moral conduct. By their observance, the yogi avoids the primary or fundamental difficulties that could block his progress toward Self-realization. Breaking the rules of moral conduct creates not only present misery, but long-lasting karmic effects that bind the devotee to suffering and mortal limitation.

Dhrishtaketu, Power of Mental Resistance, battles the desires to indulge in behavior that is contrary to spiritual law, and helps to neutralize the karmic effects of past mistakes.

8. Shaibya—Power of Mental Adherence (Niyama)

Shaibya, often written *Shaivya,* relates to Shiva, which word in turn derives from the Sanskrit root *śī,* "in whom all things lie." Shiva also means "auspicious, benevolent, happy; welfare." The metaphorical derivation of Shaibya: *Śivaṁ maṅgalaṁ tat-sambandhī-yam iti maṅgala-dāyakaṁ*— "One who adheres to what is good or auspicious—to what is conducive to one's welfare." Shaibya corresponds to Patanjali's *niyama,* religious observances. It represents the devotee's power to adhere to the spiritual prescriptions of *niyama,* the "thou shalts": purity of body and mind, contentment in all circumstances, self-discipline, self-study (contemplation), and devotion to God.

Shaibya, Power of Mental Adherence, provides the yogi with an army of positive spiritual self-discipline to defeat the battalions of evil misery-producing ways and the effects of past bad karma.

Yama-niyama are the foundation on which the yogi begins to build his spiritual life. They harmonize body and mind with the divine laws of nature, or creation, producing an inner and outer well-being, happiness, and strength that attract the devotee to deeper spiritual practices and make him receptive to the blessings of his guru-given *sadhana* (spiritual path).

9. Kuntibhoja — Right Posture (Asana)

Bhoja, in Kuntibhoja, derives from *bhuj*, "to take possession of, to rule or govern." Kuntibhoja is the adoptive father of Kunti. The metaphorical derivation: *Yena kuntiṁ kunā āmantraṇā daiva-vibhūtī ākarṣikā śaktiṁ bhunakti pālayate yaḥ saḥ* — "He who takes possession of and supports the spiritual force—Kunti—by which divine powers are invoked and drawn to oneself." Kunti is the wife of Pandu and mother of the three elder Pandava brothers—Yudhisthira, Bhima, and Arjuna—and stepmother to the two younger brothers, twins—Nakula and Sahadeva. She had the power to invoke the gods (cosmic creative forces), and through this means these five sons were born. Metaphorically, Kunti (from *ku*, to call) is the ardent devotee's spiritual power to invoke the aid of the creative life force in his *sadhana*. Kunti (as does Drupada) represents the devotee's dispassion for the world and longing for God which, during meditation, reverses the outward flowing life force to concentrate within. When the life force and consciousness are united to Pandu, *buddhi* (discrimination), the *tattvas* or elements in the subtle spinal centers (conceived in the microcosmic womb or centers of the body by the macrocosmic or universal creative forces) become manifested to the yogi (that is, are given birth to by Kunti).

Kuntibhoja represents Patanjali's *asana*, the faculty derived from the poise or control of the body, for the correct posture is essential to the yogi's practice of life-force control. As Kuntibhoja "adopted and reared"

Kunti, so does *asana* "support" the ability to invoke divine life energy in preparation for the practice of *pranayama,* or life-force control (the step following *asana* on the Eightfold Path).

Asana prescribes the necessary correct posture for yoga meditation. Though many variations have evolved, the essential basics are a steady body with straight, erect spine; chin parallel to the ground; shoulders back, chest out, abdomen in; and eyes focused at the *Kutastha* center between the eyebrows. The body must be still and unmoving, without strain or tension. When mastered, the correct posture or *asana* becomes as expressed by Patanjali, "steady and pleasant." It bestows bodily control and mental and physical calmness, enabling the yogi to meditate for hours, if so desired, without fatigue or restlessness.

It is evident, then, why *asana* is essential to life-force control: It supports the inner dispassion toward the demands of the body and the ardent power necessary to invoke the aid of the life energies in turning the consciousness inward to the world of Spirit.

Kuntibhoja, Right Posture, provides the physical and mental pacification necessary to fight the body-bound tendencies toward laziness, restlessness, and flesh attachment.

10. Yudhamanyu—Life-force Control (Pranayama)

From *yudh*, "to fight," and *manyu,* "high spirit or ardor," Yudhamanyu means "he who fights with great zeal and determination." The metaphorical derivation: *Yudham caitanya-prakāśayitum eva manu-kriyā yasya saḥ*—"One whose chief action is to fight to manifest divine consciousness." The life force is the link between matter and Spirit. Flowing outward it reveals the spuriously alluring world of the senses; reversed inward it pulls the consciousness to the eternally satisfying bliss of God. The meditating devotee sits between these two worlds, striving to enter the kingdom of God, but kept engaged in battling the senses. With the aid of a scientific technique of *pranayama* [such as *Kriya Yoga*], the yogi is at last victorious in reversing the outward-flowing life energy that externalized his consciousness in the action of breath, heart, and sense-ensnared life currents. He enters the natural inner calm realm of the soul and Spirit.

Yudhamanyu, Life-Force Control, is the invaluable warrior in the Pandava army that disarms and renders powerless the sense army of the blind mind.

11. Purujit—Interiorization (Pratyahara)

Purujit, translated literally, means "conquering many," from *puru* (root *pṛī*), "many," and *jit* (root *ji*), "conquering; removing (in meditation)." The metaphorical derivation: *Paurān indriya-adhiṣṭhātṛ-devān jayati iti*—"One who has conquered the fortresses of the astral powers ruling the senses." The Sanskrit word *pur* (root *pṛī*) means "fortress" and here refers to the sensory strongholds of the mind (*manas*) and its sensory organs, the functions of which are governed by the astral powers in the subtle cerebrospinal centers. In the Sanskrit root *ji* is the meaning "subdue, master." Purujit, as referred to in the Gita context, implies the one by which the many (the sense soldiers) of the sensory fortresses of the body are mastered or subdued. That is, Purujit represents Patanjali's *pratyahara,* the withdrawal of consciousness from the senses, the result of successful practice of *pranayama* or control of the life force (the astral powers) that enlivens the senses and bears their messages to the brain. When the devotee has attained *pratyahara,* the life is switched off from the senses, and the mind and consciousness are still and interiorized.

Purujit, Interiorization, provides the yogi with that steadiness of mental calm that prevents the prenatal habits of the sense army from causing sudden scattering of the mind on the material world.

12. Saubhadra, i.e., Son of Subhadra (Abhimanyu)—Self-mastery (Samyama)

Subhadra is the wife of Arjuna. Their son's name is Abhimanyu, from *abhi,* "with intensity; toward, into," and *manyu,* "spirit, mood, mind; ardor." Abhimanyu represents the intense mental state (one's spiritual mood, or *bhava*) in which the consciousness is drawn "toward" or "into" union with the object of its concentration or ardor, giving perfect self-control or self-mastery. It is referred to by Patanjali in his *Yoga Sutras,* III:1–4, as *samyama,* a collective term under which the last three steps of the Eightfold Path are grouped together.

The first five steps are the preliminaries of yoga. *Samyama,* from *sam,* "together," and *yama,* "holding," consists of the occult trio, *dharana* (concentration), *dhyana* (meditation), and *samadhi* (divine union), and is yoga proper. When the mind has been withdrawn from sensory disturbances (*pratyahara*), then *dharana* and *dhyana* in conjunction produce the varying stages of *samadhi:* ecstatic realization and, finally, divine union. *Dhyana,* or meditation, is the focusing of the freed attention on Spirit. It involves the meditator, the process or technique of meditation, and the object of meditation. *Dharana* is concentration or fixity on that inner conception or object of meditation. Thus arises from this contemplation the perception of the Divine Presence, first within oneself, and then evolving into cosmic conception—conceiving of the vastness of Spirit, omnipresent within and beyond all creation. The culmination of *samyama* self-mastery is when the meditator, the process of meditating, and the object of meditation become one—the full realization of oneness with Spirit.

By reference in the Gita text to Abhimanyu's metronymic, Saubhadra, we are directed to the meaning of Subhadra, "glorious, splendid." Thus Abhimanyu is that self-mastery which bestows light or illumination. The metaphorical derivation: *Abhi sarvatra manute prakāśate iti*—"One whose intensely concentrating mind shines everywhere," i.e., lights or reveals everything; makes manifest the illumined state of Self-realization.

Abhimanyu, Self-Mastery, is that great Pandava warrior whose victories enable the yogi to hold back the onslaught of the restless, delusive consciousness of ego, senses, and habits and thus to remain longer and longer in the state of divine soul consciousness—both during and after meditation.

13. Sons of Draupadi—Five Spinal Centers Awakened by Kundalini

Draupadi is the daughter of Drupada (Extreme Dispassion). She represents the spiritual power or feeling of *kundalini,* which is roused, or born of, the Drupada divine ardor and dispassion. When *kundalini* is lifted upward, it is "wedded" to the five Pandavas (the creative vibratory elements and consciousness in the five spinal centers), and thereby gives birth to five sons.*

The sons of Draupadi are the manifestations of the five opened or awakened spinal centers—such as the specific forms, lights, or sounds characteristic of each center—upon which the yogi concentrates to draw divine discriminative power to fight the sense mind and its offspring.

---

* Part of the story of Draupadi in the *Mahabharata* is recounted by Paramahansa Yogananda as follows: "In an elaborate ceremony called *svayamvara,* held by King Drupada to choose a husband for his daughter Draupadi, Drupada made the condition that the hand of his daughter would be given only to the prince who could bend a gigantic bow provided for the occasion, and with it hit the eye of a cleverly concealed and suspended target. Princes from far and near tried and failed even to lift the bow. Arjuna succeeded easily. When the five Pandus returned home, their mother Kunti, hearing their approach from a distance and presuming they had won some wealth, called out to them that they must equally share their winnings. As the mother's word must be honored, Draupadi became the wife of all five brothers. She bore one son by each."

CHAPTER 4

The Psychological Forces
That Oppose the Soul

The Bhagavad Gita—a comprehensive metaphysical and psychological treatise—describes all experiences that will come to the
spiritual traveler on the path of emancipation. Thus far, concentration
has been primarily on the positive states the devotee is striving toward.
In the verses that follow...warning is given as to the negative states that
try to intimidate the devotee and turn him from his goal. "Forewarned is
forearmed!" The devotee who understands the route he must travel will
never feel unsure or dismayed at inevitable opposition.

[In verses 8–9 of the Gita's first chapter, Duryodhana (Material
Desire) relates that he is counting on the following allies to maintain his
rule of the bodily kingdom:]

*"These warriors are thyself (Drona), Bhishma, Karna, and Kripa
—victors in battles; Ashvatthaman, Vikarna, the son of Somadatta,
and Jayadratha.*

*"And numerous other warriors, all well-trained for battle and
armed with various weapons, are here present, ready for my sake
to lay down their lives."*

As the Pandavas enumerated in verses 4–6 represent the principles necessary for the yogi to attain realization or oneness with God, the Kauravas
named by Duryodhana in verse 8 are metaphorically representative of specific principles that oppose spiritual progress.

In the *Yoga Sutras*, I:24, Patanjali says: "The Lord (Ishvara) is untouched by *klesha* (troubles), *karma* (action), *vipaka* (habit), and *ashaya*
(desire)."

In the *Yoga Sutras*, II:3, *klesha*, or troubles, is defined as fivefold:

avidya (ignorance), *asmita* (ego), *raga* (attachment), *dvesha* (aversion), *abhinivesha* (body attachment). Since the Lord is free from these eight imperfections inherent in creation, the yogi who seeks union with God must likewise first rid his consciousness of these obstacles to spiritual victory.

When the ego or "I" consciousness has sided with the materialistic forces of creation, it is said to have six faults (*doshas*): *kama* (lust); *krodha* (anger); *lobha* (greed); *moha* (delusion); *mada* (pride); *matsarya* (envy).

[A detailed description of each of the above "psychological enemies" is given in *God Talks With Arjuna*, including the correlation of the Sanskrit name of each warrior with the quality he symbolizes. Following are a few basic points about the principal enemies of spiritual progress:]

Egoism (Symbolized by Bhishma)

The name Bhishma derives from the Sanskrit root *bhī* or *bhīṣ*, "to frighten."...In the psychological-metaphysical battle being described, Bhishma-Ego is the most powerful opponent of the Pandavas, thus igniting the greatest fear in the hearts of the spiritual forces in the spinal centers that are striving to turn toward Spirit to reestablish the kingdom of divine soul consciousness.

Patanjali's *asmita*, the second of the *kleshas*, derives from the Sanskrit *asmi*, "I am," (from *as*, to be). It is thus egoism, the same as the allegorical Bhishma in the Gita....

Patanjali describes the *klesha* of the individualized sense of being thus: "*Asmita* (egoism) is the identifying of the seer with the instruments of seeing." Ego is when the soul, or seer, the image of God in man, forgets its true divine Self and becomes identified with the powers of perception and action in the instruments of the body and mind. *Asmita* is therefore the consciousness in which the seer (the soul or its pseudonature, the ego) and its discriminating powers are present as though indivisibly one and the same.

The degree of ignorance or enlightenment inherent in this identification depends on the nature of the respective instruments through which the "I-ness" or individuality is manifesting. When identified with the gross senses and their objects (the physical body and material world), the "I-ness" becomes the wisdom-destroying physical ego. When identified with the subtle instruments of perception and knowledge in the astral body, the "I-ness" becomes a clearer sense of being, the astral ego, whose true nature may be adversely affected by the delusive influence of the physical nature; or, conversely, be in tune with the instrumentality of the wisdom consciousness of the causal body and thus become the discriminating ego.

When the "I-ness" expresses solely through pure intuitive wisdom, the instrument of the causal body, it becomes the pure discriminating ego (the divine ego), or its highest expression, the soul, the individualized reflection of Spirit. The soul, the purest individualized sense of being, knows its Spirit-identity of omniscience and omnipresence, and merely uses the instruments of the body and mind as a means of communication and interaction with objectified creation. Thus the Hindu scriptures say: "When this 'I' shall die, then will I know who am I."

In the context of this present verse, in which the inner metaphysical forces of the Kaurava army are described, the implication of Bhishma–Ego Consciousness is in the form of the astral, or inner-seeing ego: the consciousness identified with the subtle form of the instruments of sense mind (*manas*), intelligence (*buddhi*), and feeling (*chitta*). At this stage of the devotee's advancement, this astral or inner-seeing ego is strongly affected by the outward pull of the sense mind; that is, it has sided with the Kurus. In the victory of *samadhi,* this "I-ness" (*asmita*), inner-seeing ego, becomes more transcendent as the discriminating ego of the astral and causal bodily instruments, and ultimately as the pure individualized sense of being, the soul.

Bhishma (*asmita* or delusion-born ego consciousness) is the supreme commander over all units of the sense army. The purpose of Bhishma, the ego or pseudosoul, is to keep the consciousness continually busy with sensory reports and activities by focusing the searchlight of attention outwardly on the body and the world of matter, instead of inwardly on God and the true soul nature. This deluded flesh-bound consciousness is responsible for awakening all the countless soldiers of temptations and attachments couched within the human body.

Without ego consciousness the entire army of evil and temptation vanishes like a forgotten dream. If the soul dwelt in the body without being identified with it, as do the souls of saints, no temptations or attachments could keep it tied to the body.

The troubles of an ordinary man arise from the fact that when the soul descends into the body, it projects its individualized, ever-conscious, ever-new-bliss nature into the flesh and thereafter identifies itself with the limitations of a physical form. The soul then thinks of itself as the miserable ego of many temptations.

The identification of the soul with the body, however, is only imaginary, not real. Essentially the soul is ever pure. Ordinary mortals allow their souls to live as flesh-entangled egos, not as Spirit's reflection or true soul.

Kama (Lust) — Symbolized by Duryodhana (Material Desire)

In the name and guise of fulfilling one's needs, ego lures man to continuous seeking of self-satisfaction, resulting in suffering and vexation. What would content the soul is forgotten, and the ego goes on endlessly trying to satisfy its insatiable desires. *Kama* (lust) is therefore the compelling desire to indulge in sensory temptations.

Coercive materialistic desire is the instigator of man's wrong thoughts and actions. Interacting with the other forces that obstruct man's divine nature — influencing as well as being influenced by them — lustful desire is the consummate enemy. The perfect exemplar is Duryodhana, whose unwillingness to part with even an inch of sensory territory or pleasure was the cause of the war of Kurukshetra. Only little by little, with fierce determination in battle, could the Pandavas win back their kingdom.

Kama, or lustful desire, supported by the other Kaurava forces, can corrupt the sensory instruments of man to expression of their basest instincts. It is taught in the Hindu scriptures that under the strong influence of *kama,* sane learned men act like asses, monkeys, goats, and swine.

Lust applies to the abuse of any or all of the senses in the pursuit of pleasure or gratification. Through the sense of sight man may lust after material objects; through the sense of hearing, he craves the sweet, slow

The Power of Pranayama in Winning the Spiritual Battle

[In chapter I verse 10, Duryodhana/Material Desire—leader of the forces of ignorance—states:]

"Our forces protected by Bhishma are unlimited (but may be insufficient); whereas their army, defended by Bhima, is limited (but quite adequate)."

Duryodhana–Material Desire knows that his kingdom is seriously threatened when the aspiring devotee begins to rouse the inner spiritual army by the practice of meditation. Bhima, the soul-guided vital force, is the primary general of this army, for life force is the link between matter and Spirit; no realization is possible until this energy is brought under control and turned toward Spirit.

As the meditating devotee becomes adept in the proper *pranayama* techniques [such as *Kriya Yoga*], Bhima, the inwardly turned life force and resultant life and breath control, leads that victorious yogi to divine consciousness....When life force is shut off from the sensory organs, material sensations cannot reach the brain to snatch away the meditator's attention from God. This is why Bhima, or the power of life-force control, and a few other strong soldiers—concentration, intuition, inner perception, calmness, self-control, and so on (as described in verses 4–6)—must be awakened to fight the forces of the pseudosoul or ego.

Bhima, or soul-guided life force, heads the spiritual army and is the principal enemy of ego or Bhishma, because when the invasion of the five senses is halted by life-force control, the soul is automatically freed from the captivity of the body-identified ego-consciousness. The soul, having regained supreme command of the consciousness, says: "I was never anything but joyous Spirit; I only imagined for a time that I was mortal man being imprisoned by delusive limitations and sensory temptations."

This "awakening" of the soul, or Self-realization, occurs first as a temporary awareness during the experience of *samadhi* in deep meditation, after successful practice of *pranayama* has produced life-force control and reversed the life and consciousness from the senses to the divine inner states of soul- and God-awareness. As the yogi's *samadhi* experiences deepen and expand, this realization becomes a permanent state of consciousness.

Attaining *samadhi* or oneness with God is the only method by which the ego consciousness can be completely defeated.

poison of flattery, and vibratory sounds as of voices and music that rouse his material nature; through the lustful pleasure of smell he is enticed toward wrong environments and actions; lust for food and drink causes him to please his taste at the expense of health; through the sense of touch he lusts after inordinate physical comfort and abuses the creative sex impulse.

Lust also seeks gratification in wealth, status, power, domination—all that satisfies the "I, me, mine" in the egotistical man.

Lustful desire is egotism, the lowest rung of the ladder of human character evolution. By the force of its insatiable passion, *kama* loves to destroy one's happiness, health, brain power, clarity of thought, memory, and discriminative judgment.

The Good and Bad Power of Habit (Symbolized by Drona)

Very seldom does man realize that his health, success, and wisdom depend in great part on the issue of the battle between his good and bad habits. He who would establish within himself the rule of the soul must not allow the bodily kingdom to be occupied by bad habits. All such evils must be banished by training diverse good habits in the art of victorious psychological warfare.

❖ ❖ ❖

The name Drona comes from the Sanskrit root *dru*, "to melt." Therefore, Drona implies "that which remains in a melted state." A thought or physical act once performed does not cease to be, but remains in the consciousness in a more subtle or "melted" form as an impression of that gross expression of thought or action. These impressions are called *samskaras*. They create strong inner urges, tendencies, or propensities that influence the intelligence to repeat those thoughts and actions. Oft-repeated, such impulses become compelling habits. Thus, we may simplify the translation of *samskara* in this context as inner tendency or urge, or habit. The preceptor Drona symbolizes *samskara*, broadly defined as inner tendency, or habit.

According to the historical story in the *Mahabharata*, Drona was the masterly preceptor who had taught archery to both the Kurus and the Pandavas. During the battle between the two parties, however, Drona sided with the Kurus.

The good discriminative tendencies of the soul's pure intelligence (*buddhi*) and the wicked mental tendencies of the sense mind (*manas*) had both learned from Inner Tendency, Drona, the battle arts of wielding, respectively, the weapons of soul-revealing wisdom, and of truth-obscuring sense consciousness.

The subconscious urges of one's *samskaras,* if good, help to create present good thoughts, actions, and habits. When these innate urges are evil, they rouse wicked thoughts that turn into evil actions and habits. Just as a bird turns its head to focus one eye at a time on a given object, so Drona, the *samskara-* or habit-guided intelligence, uses one-sided vision and supports the dominant tendencies. This Drona, inner urge, joins the wicked mental tendencies (Kurus) when they are predominant in a man. Therefore, unless *samskara,* or the sense-habit inclination, is purified by wisdom, it will be found to be a follower of Duryodhana, or King Material Desire. This is why, in the devotee who has yet to win the victory in the battle of Kurukshetra, Drona or the bad-habit-influenced intelligence joins the side of the Kurus or the wicked mental tendencies, helping them to direct their arrows of piercing evil against the discriminative powers.

In sum, the principal practical evil that comes along with ego consciousness and its six faults is the increasing compulsion to forget one's Self—the soul—and its expression, manifestation, and requirements; and to become stubbornly inclined to engage oneself in pursuing the insatiable "necessities" of the ego.

Psychologically, ego consciousness is a transference and grafting of a false personality. It is necessary to understand and uproot the picketing of ego consciousness and its various tendencies, which preclude familiarity with the true Self.

The aspiring yogi should always bear in mind, when he feels angry, "That is not me!" When his self-possession is being overpowered by lust or greed, he should say to himself, "That is not me!" When hatred tries to obscure his real nature with a mask of ugly emotion, he should forcefully dissociate himself from it: "That is not me!" He learns to shut the doors of his consciousness against all undesirable visitors seeking lodging within.

And whenever that devotee has been used or abused by others, and yet he feels within a stirring of the holy spirit of forgiveness and love, he can then affirm with conviction, "*That* is me! That is my real nature."

Yoga meditation is the process of cultivating and stabilizing the awareness of one's real nature, through definite spiritual and psychophysical methods and laws by which the narrow ego, the flawed hereditary human consciousness, is displaced by the consciousness of the soul.*

Each worldly person, moralist, spiritual aspirant, and yogi—like a devotee—should every night before retiring ask his intuition whether his spiritual faculties or his physical inclinations of temptation won the day's battles:

- between good and bad habits;
- between temperance and greed;
- between self-control and lust;
- between honest desire for necessary money and inordinate craving for gold;
- between forgiveness and anger;
- between joy and grief;
- between moroseness and pleasantness;
- between kindness and cruelty;
- between selfishness and unselfishness;
- between understanding and jealousy;
- between bravery and cowardice;
- between confidence and fear;
- between faith and doubt;
- between humbleness and pride;
- between desire to commune with God in meditation and the restless urge for worldly activities;
- between spiritual and material desires;
- between divine ecstasy and sensory perceptions;
- between soul consciousness and egoity.

---

* The noble qualities expressed by one who is awakening soul consciousness are described by Lord Krishna in the opening verses of chapter XVI of the Bhagavad Gita. See page 140.

CHAPTER 5

The Triumph of the Soul
Through Practice of Yoga

[In Bhagavad Gita VI:5–6, Lord Krishna counsels Arjuna:]

"Let man uplift the self (ego) by the self; let the self not be self-degraded (cast down). Indeed, the self is its own friend; and the self is its own enemy.

"For him whose self (ego) has been conquered by the Self (soul), the Self is the friend of the self; but verily, the Self behaves inimically, as an enemy, toward the self that is not subdued."

The physical ego, the active consciousness in man, should uplift its body-identified self into unity with the soul, its true nature; it should not allow itself to remain mired in the lowly delusive strata of the senses and material entanglement. The ego acts as its own best friend when by meditation and the exercise of its innate soul qualities it spiritualizes itself and ultimately restores its own true soul nature. Conversely, the physical ego serves as its own worst enemy when by delusive material behavior it eclipses its true nature as the ever blessed soul.

When the physical ego (the active consciousness) has become spiritualized and united to the soul, it is able to keep the intelligence, mind, and senses under control, guided by the discriminative wisdom of the soul—i.e., the "self (ego) has been conquered by the Self (soul)"—then the soul is the friend, the guide and benefactor, of the active physical consciousness.

But if the lower ego-self has not been thus controlled and persists in keeping the consciousness matter-bent, then the soul is the enemy of the ego. This follows the Gita allegory described in chapter one: Krishna (the soul) is the friend and guide of the spiritual endeavors of the devotee

Arjuna, along with the Pandava army of divine qualities; Krishna (the soul) is therefore an enemy (an opposer) of Duryodhana's Kaurava army of materialistic inclinations, which is under the guidance of Bhishma (ego).

The soul, "inimical" to the ego, withholds its blessings of peace and lasting happiness while the ego, behaving ignorantly as its own enemy, sets in motion the misery-making karmic forces of Nature. Without the beneficence of the soul's protection in the world of *maya*, the ego finds to its regret that its own actions against its true soul nature turn back on itself, like boomerangs, destroying each new illusion of happiness and attainment.

In the composition of these two concise verses, the word *atman* ("self") appears twelve times in an ambiguous construction allowing for the interchange of meaning either as "the soul" or "the ego" (the pseudosoul)—a classical example of the dichotomy so characteristic in Indian scripture. As shown in the above commentary, the clever interweavings of the words *soul* and *ego* in this instance consist of a singular thread of truth that runs through the whole fabric of the Gita: Let man be uplifted, not degraded; let him transform his self (ego) into the Self (soul). The Self is the friend of the transformed self, but the enemy of the unregenerate self.

[Sri Krishna continues in VI:46:]

"The yogi is deemed greater than body-disciplining ascetics, greater even than the followers of the path of wisdom or of the path of action; be thou, O Arjuna, a yogi!"

Various methods and bypaths are termed yoga: *Karma Yoga* (the path of good actions); *Jnana Yoga* (the path of discrimination); *Bhakti Yoga* (the path of prayer and devotion); *Mantra Yoga* (the path of God-union by chanting and incantations of seed sounds); *Laya Yoga* (the path that teaches how to dissolve the ego in the Infinite); and *Hatha Yoga* (the path of bodily discipline). *Raja Yoga*, specifically *Kriya Yoga*, is the quintessence of all yoga paths, the path especially favored by royal sages and great yogis in ancient India.

Raja Yoga: The Highest Path

The Lord Himself here extols the royal path of yoga as the highest of all spiritual paths, and the scientific yogi as greater than a follower of any other path.

The real *Kriya Yoga* way (life-force control) is not a bypath. It is the direct highway, the shortest route, to divine realization. It teaches man to ascend heavenward by leading the ego, mind, and life force through the same spinal channel that was used when the soul originally descended into the body.

The Spirit as soul has descended through the subtle astral cerebrospinal centers into the brain and the spinal plexuses, and into the nervous system, the senses, and the rest of the body, and becomes entangled there as the pseudosoul or ego. In the body-identified state, the ego engages in further involvements in and with the objective world. The ego has to be made to ascend through the same spinal path until it realizes its true Self as the soul, and the soul reunites with the Spirit.

Yoga points out that this spinal route is the one straight highway that all earth-descended mortal beings must follow in the final ascension to liberation. All other paths—those that emphasize performance of *tapasya* (bodily and mental self-discipline), or theoretical knowledge of the scriptures (the gaining of wisdom by discrimination), or the performance of all good actions—are auxiliary paths that somewhere join the highway of practical yoga that leads straight to liberation.

Outer Renunciation, Scriptural Study, and Serviceful Action Are Bypaths

The ascetic who is busy with disciplining the body, putting it through rigorous austerities, may attain a degree of control over the physical instrumentality; but merely practicing postures, enduring cold and heat, and not giving in to sorrow and pleasure—without simultaneously concentrating on Cosmic Consciousness—is only a roundabout pathway to gaining the mental control necessary for God-communion. The yogi attains communion with the Lord directly, by withdrawing his consciousness from the senses and nervous system, the spine, and the brain, and uniting it with his God-knowing soul. Many devotees are so engrossed in following the precepts of external asceticism and renunciation that they forget that ecstasy with the Infinite is the purpose of such self-discipline.

When the scriptural philosopher dissects words and thoughts with the scalpel of his reason, he may grow so fond of theoretical knowledge and of mentally separating wisdom into various segments that he may "dry up" through lack of the experience of truth in divine ecstasy. If a person spent his lifetime in analyzing the properties of water and in examining water from different sources all over the world, he would not thereby quench his thirst. A thirsty man, without fussing over the atomic constituencies, selects some good water; drinking it, he becomes satisfied. An exoteric *jnana yogi*—a follower of the path of discriminative reason—may read and analyze all the scriptures and still not slake his soul thirst.

A theoretical knowledge of scriptures often produces a conviction that one knows the truth when he actually does not know it. Only by communing with God, the "Library of All Knowledge," may one know all truths in their exactitude, without wasting time in the theoretical understanding and misunderstanding of scriptures. That is why a wide gulf may exist between scripture readers and men of realization who are themselves embodiments of scriptural truths.

The Pharisees were willing to crucify Christ because they surmised fearfully that he was a threat to their authority, having actually perceived the truths that they knew only in theory.

Lastly, the yogi is also deemed greater than the man of action. The missionary, the social worker, the man of goodwill who practices the "golden rule" toward others, the teacher who tries to instruct others in the technique of God-communion—all no doubt perform good actions. But unless they also devote themselves to the inner science by which they can know God through their own direct experience, they will remain without divine realization.

That is why the yogi meditates and concentrates on the attainment of ecstasy. Until he achieves that state of inner attunement with God, he performs his duties but does not divert himself with many outward activities at the cost of forgetting the Lord.

The yogi teaches and serves others in the highest way—by his inspiring life; example ever speaks louder than words. Reform thyself and thou wilt reform thousands. Forgetting God is the greatest sin. Communion with God is the highest virtue.

A little study of scriptures with the continuous desire to practice the truths enjoined in them is desirable in the path of yoga. Renunciation of all entanglements in order to commune with God is also helpful. Performance of dutiful actions that satisfy one's own needs and that are serviceful and uplifting to others provides a beneficial balance in the life of the yogi.

Raja Yoga Is the True Culmination of All Religious Practices

The paths of renunciation and wisdom and action may be followed in two ways: externally and internally. The man who concentrates on external renunciation is an outer renunciant. But the *tapasvin* [ascetic] who destroys all internal desires and attachments, and who keeps his mind away from sense temptations, is a man of esoteric renunciation.

Similarly, the external follower of the wisdom path (*Jnana Yoga*) is busy in solving scriptural problems and in analyzing word structures. The esoteric *jnanin*, according to Vedanta philosophy, is he who not only listens to the scriptural truths and perceives their meaning in his mind but becomes one with them by complete assimilation. Therefore the Vedantic way of spiritual realization is to listen to the scriptural truth (*shravanam*), then to perceive it (*mananam*), then to be one with it (*nididhyasanam*).

The man who performs good actions is the external *karma yogi*. He who practices yoga meditation performs the highest action; he is the esoteric *karmin*. But he who performs or practices *Kriya Yoga*, the highest technique of contacting God, is the *raja yogi* or the royal *Kriya Yogi*. He attains ascension and is thus among the highest yogis.

Kriya Yoga: The Essential Technique of Raja Yoga

Another interpretation of this stanza has been given by Lahiri Mahasaya: When a yogi practices *Kriya Yoga*, withdrawing his mind from the senses by disconnecting the life force from the five sense-telephones, he is spoken of as following the path of *karma yoga;* he is a true *karmin*. During this earlier state of attempts at God-union, the yogi has to perform various spiritual actions of proper breathing, life-force control, and fighting distractions with concentration. Therefore he is spoken of as following the path of esoteric *karma yoga*. At this state the yogi is identified with actions; he is a *karmin*.

When the yogi is able to see the spiritual light at the *Kutastha* or Christ center between the eyebrows and to withdraw his life force from the nervous system of the five sense-telephones, he enters the state of esoteric *tapasya* (ascetical renunciation). His mind, being disconnected from the senses, then exists in a state of esoteric renunciation; he is a *tapasvin*.

When the yogi is further able to unite his mind with the wisdom and bliss of his soul, he is a follower of esoteric *Jnana Yoga*. This is called the *jnanin* state of the yogi.

In the last high state when the soul, free from all bodily and world-ly consciousness, is united with the blessed Cosmic Spirit, the devotee is called the esoteric *raja yogi*. This state of final yoga or union of soul and Spirit is the loftiest; he who attains it is the true yogi. He has reached higher spiritual planes than the one who has achieved only the state of a *tapasvin, karmin,* or *jnanin*. The real yogi knows God as the ever-existing, ever-conscious, ever-new Bliss; he perceives all creation as God's dreams.

The path of *Kriya Yoga* is distinctive and scientific because it teaches the exact method of withdrawing the mind from the senses by switch-ing off the life force from the five sense-telephones. Only when this inte-riorization is accomplished can the meditator enter the inner temple of God-communion. In other words, the *Kriya Yogi* follows a sure, definite method of leading not only his mind but his life force through the spinal channel to unite them with the soul. In the highest ecstasy he then unites his soul with Spirit.

Kriya Yoga, or the indirect reference to it in the scriptures as *Kevali Pranayama,** is the true *pranayama*, in which the inhaling and exhal-ing breath has been transmuted into interiorized life force under the full

---

* Explained in *God Talks With Arjuna*, Chapter 4, verse 29.

control of the mind. By distilling *prana* from the breath, and by neutralizing the life currents that control the breath, all the cells of the body are vitally recharged by the reinforced bodily life force and the Cosmic Life; the physical cells neither change nor decay. *Kriya Yoga* is a suitable practice for any sincere seeker of God who is free from serious acute illness, and who observes in his daily life the cardinal moral precepts.*

The theologies of all great religions have one common foundation—the finding of God. But religious truth without practical realization is necessarily limited in its value. How can the blind lead the blind? Few men understand the Bhagavad Gita as its writer, Vyasa, understood its truths! Few men understand the words of Christ as he understood them!

Vyasa, Christ, Babaji, and all other perfected masters perceived the same truth. They described it variously, in different languages. In the study of the Bhagavad Gita and the New Testament I have perceived their meanings as one....

In order to understand fully the Bhagavad Gita and the Bible, the spiritual aspirant must learn to go into the state of ecstasy and commune with Vyasa and Christ through Cosmic Consciousness.

As all colleges in the world teach the same principles of science, which can be proven by application, so all true religious schools, if they followed yoga, would be aware that it is the one scientific highway to the Infinite. That is why each man should become a God-united yogi. In this stanza of the Bhagavad Gita, the voice of God sounds a trumpet call to all spiritual aspirants: Become yogis!

The Reign of King Soul in the Spiritualized Bodily Kingdom

The deeper the yogi's meditations, and the more he is able to hold on to the aftereffects of awakened soul-virtues and perceptions and express them in his daily life, the more spiritualized his bodily kingdom becomes. His unfolding Self-realization is the triumphal reestablishing of the reign of King Soul. Amazing changes take place within an ordinary man when

---

*Detailed instruction in the actual techniques of *Kriya Yoga* is given to students of the *Self-Realization Fellowship Lessons* who fulfill the requirements of certain preliminary spiritual disciplines. See page 165.

King Soul and his noble courtiers of intuition, peace, bliss, calmness, self-control, life-force control, will power, concentration, discrimination, omniscience, rule the bodily kingdom!

The yogi who has won the battle of consciousness has overcome the misguided ego's attachment to human titles, such as, "I am a man, an American, with so many pounds of flesh, a millionaire of this city," and so on, and has released the prisoner of his attention from all limiting delusion. His freed attention, which beheld creation only through the restrictive outer searchlights of the senses, withdraws into an infinite kingdom seen only through the searchlights of inner perception....The inwardly reversed searchlights of perception reveal to the yogi the hiding place of the ever beautiful, ever joyous Spirit in all creation....

The man into whose pure hand his divine bodily kingdom has been wholly delivered is no longer a human being with limited ego consciousness. In reality, he is the soul, individualized ever-existent, ever-conscious, ever-new Bliss, the pure reflection of Spirit, endowed with cosmic consciousness....

He feels by true intuitive power the ever-bubbling Bliss that dances in every particle of his little body, and in his big Cosmic Body of the universe, and in his absolute nature as one with the Eternal Spirit beyond manifested forms....

This is Self-realization, man's native state as the soul, the pure reflection of Spirit. Dreams of incarnations play on the delusive screen of individuality; but in reality, never for a moment is man separate from God. We are His thought; He is our being. From Him we have come. In Him we are to live as expressions of His wisdom, His love, His joy. In Him our egoity must melt again, in the ever-wakeful dreamlessness of eternal Bliss.

Symbolically, then, this is the scene as the Gita dialogue commences: Man's soul consciousness—the realization of his oneness with the eternal, all-blissful Spirit—has descended through various gradations into mortal body-consciousness.* The senses and blind mind, and the power

---

* Symbolized by Shantanu and his wives and descendants, as cited on page 6.

  As mentioned in the Preface, many Gita verses have a literal meaning as well as a deeper sym-

of pure discrimination, both reign in the bodily kingdom; there is constant conflict between the forces of the materialistic senses (engaging the consciousness in the pursuit of external pleasure) and the pure discriminative power that tries to return man's consciousness to its native state of soul-realization....

Each person has to fight his own battle of Kurukshetra. It is a war not only worth winning, but in the divine order of the universe and of the eternal relationship between the soul and God, a war that sooner or later must be won.

In the holy Bhagavad Gita, the quickest attainment of that victory is assured to the devotee who, through undiscourageable practice of the divine science of yoga meditation, learns like Arjuna to hearken to the inner wisdom-song of Spirit.

---

bolic meaning. The symbology cited in the foregoing pages will enable the reader to appreciate the hidden metaphorical meanings in many of the verses when reading the translation presented in Part II. Other verses, not explained in this brief work, can be easily understood in their literal sense, but Paramahansa Yogananda's commentary in *God Talks With Arjuna* should be studied for a full comprehension. *(Publisher's Note)*

PART II

THE
BHAGAVAD GITA

Original translation by
Paramahansa Yogananda

NOTE: Throughout the Gita dialogue, Lord Krishna and his disciple Arjuna are referred to by numerous epithets, such as Keshava (Krishna) or Partha (Arjuna). The meaning of each epithet is given in a list on pages 158–59. The reason a particular epithet is used in a given verse (to convey a philosophical point) is explained in the commentary for those verses in *God Talks With Arjuna. (Publisher's Note)*

Sanjaya (symbolizing the power of impartial introspection) informs the blind King Dhritarashtra (the lower sensory mind) about the events of the Kurukshetra War—the spiritual battle between the psychological forces of material ignorance and the forces of the higher discriminative mind and soul.

CHAPTER I

The Despondency of Arjuna

The Opposing Armies of the Spiritual and Materialistic Forces

Dhritarashtra said:

On the holy plain of Kurukshetra (*dharmakshetra kurukshetra*), when my offspring and the sons of Pandu had gathered together, eager for battle, what did they, O Sanjaya?   1

Sanjaya said:

Then King Duryodhana, after having seen the armies of the Pandavas in battle array, repaired to his preceptor (Drona), and spoke as follows: 2

O Teacher, behold this great army of the sons of Pandu, arranged in battle order by thy talented disciple, the son of Drupada.   3

Here present are mighty heroes, extraordinary bowmen as skillful in battle as Bhima and Arjuna — the veteran warriors, Yuyudhana, Virata, and Drupada; the powerful Dhrishtaketu, Chekitana, and Kashiraja; eminent among men, Purujit; and Kuntibhoja, and Shaibya; the strong Yudhamanyu, the valiant Uttamaujas, the son of Subhadra, and the sons of Draupadi — all lords of great chariots.*   4 – 6

Listen, too, O Flower of the twice-born (best of the Brahmins), about the generals of my army who are prominent amongst ourselves: these I speak about now for thine information.   7

These warriors are thyself (Drona), Bhishma, Karna, and Kripa —victors in battles; Ashvatthaman, Vikarna, the son of Somadatta, and Jayadratha.   8

---

* *Mahāratha,* "great chariot-warrior" (*mahā,* from *mahat,* "great, lordly, kingly"; *ratha,* "chariot, warrior") denotes one who is highly skilled in the science of battle, commanding thousands of men, and able singlehandedly to fight ten thousand archers at one time.

And numerous other warriors, all well-trained for battle and armed with various weapons, are here present, ready for my sake to lay down their lives.   9

These our forces protected by Bhishma are unlimited (but may be insufficient); whereas their army, defended by Bhima, is limited (but quite adequate).*   10

All of you, properly stationed in your places in the divisions of the army, do protect Bhishma.   11

Grandsire Bhishma, oldest and most powerful of the Kurus, with the purpose of cheering Duryodhana, blew his conch shell with a re-sounding lion's roar.   12

Then suddenly (after Bhishma's first note), a great chorus from conch shells, kettledrums, cymbals, tabors, and cowhorn-trumpets sounded (from the side of the Kurus); the noise was terrific. 13

Then also, Madhava (Krishna) and Pandava (Arjuna), seated in their grand chariot with its yoke of white horses, splendidly blew their celestial conch shells.   14

Hrishikesha (Krishna) blew his Panchajanya; Dhananjaya (Arjuna), his Devadatta; and Vrikodara (Bhima), of terrible deeds, blew his great conch Paundra.   15

King Yudhisthira, the son of Kunti, blew his Anantavijaya; Nakula and Sahadeva blew, respectively, their Sughosha and Manipushpaka. 16

The King of Kashi, excellent archer; Sikhandi, the great warrior; Dhrishtadyumna, Virata, the invincible Satyaki, Drupada, the sons of Draupadi, and the mighty-armed son of Subhadra, all blew their own conches, O Lord of Earth.   17–18

That tremendous sound reverberating throughout heaven and earth pierced the heart of the Dhritarashtra clan.   19

---

*The Sanskrit words *aparyāptaṁ* and *paryāptaṁ* mean not only unlimited and limited respectively, but also the opposite implication of insufficient or inadequate, and sufficient or adequate. Either translation is tenable if the intent is understood. One principle of truth—being uncondi-tioned and eternal—if rightly applied, is capable of routing a horde of evil tendencies whose rel-ative existence depends on the temporal nature of delusion.

The Devotee Observes the Enemies to Be Destroyed

Beholding the dynasty of Dhritarashtra ready to begin battle, Pandava (Arjuna), he whose flag bears the monkey emblem, lifted his bow and addressed Hrishikesha (Krishna). (20)

Arjuna said:

O Changeless Krishna, please place my chariot between the two armies, that I may regard those who stand ready in battle array. On the eve of this war, let me comprehend with whom I must fight. (21–22)

Here in this field (of Kurukshetra) I wish to observe all those who have gathered with desire to fight on the side of Dhritarashtra's wicked son (Duryodhana). (23)

Sanjaya said (to Dhritarashtra):

O descendant of Bharata, requested thus by Gudakesha (Arjuna), Hrishikesha (Krishna) drove that best of chariots to a point between

---

Yogic Symbolism of the Sounding of the Conch Shells

In these verses reference is made to the specific vibratory sounds (the conch shells of the various Pandavas) the meditating devotee hears emanating from the astral centers in the spine and medulla. *Pranava,* the sound of the creative *Aum* vibration, is the mother of all sounds. The intelligent cosmic energy of *Aum* that issues forth from God, and is the manifestation of God, is the creator and substance of all matter. This holy vibration is the link between matter and Spirit. Meditation on *Aum* is the way to realize the true Spirit-essence of all creation. By inwardly following the sound of *Pranava* to its source, the yogi's consciousness is carried aloft to God.

In the microcosmic universe of the body of man, the *Aum* vibration works through the vital activities in the astral spinal centers of life with their creative vibratory elements (*tattvas*) of earth, water, fire, air, and ether. Through these, man's body is created, enlivened, and sustained. These vibrations emit characteristic variations of *Pranava* as they operate. The devotee whose consciousness becomes attuned to these inner astral sounds [through techniques of yoga meditation] finds himself gradually ascending to higher states of realization.

the two armies, in front of Bhishma, Drona, and all the rulers of the earth, and then said: "See, Partha (Arjuna), this gathering of all the Kurus!"   24–25

Partha (Arjuna) beheld positioned there — as members of both armies — grandfathers, fathers, fathers-in-law, uncles, brothers and cousins, sons, and grandsons, and also comrades, friends, and teachers.   26

Arjuna's Refusal to Fight

Beholding all those relatives arrayed before him, the son of Kunti (Arjuna) became filled with deep sympathy and spoke dolefully: 27

O Krishna, seeing these, my relatives, met together desirous of battle, my limbs are failing and my mouth is parched. My body trembles; my hair stands on end. The sacred bow Gandiva slips away from my grip, and my skin is afire. Neither can I remain standing upright. My mind is rambling; and, O Keshava (Krishna), I behold evil omens.   28–30

O Krishna, neither do I perceive any worthwhile effect in slaying my own kinsmen in the battle. I crave neither triumph, nor kingdom, nor pleasures!   31

Of what use to us is dominion; of what avail happiness or even the

The Nature of Arjuna's Despondency

The devotee, following the path of meditation in hope of complete emancipation, realizes that he has to destroy his material tendencies because they militate against the pursuance of the superior soul pleasures. But because of his long familial relationship with these tendencies, he becomes dejected at the prospect and is spoken of as feeling sympathetic toward these dear psychological relatives. What mortal does not feel this tender compassion for self? After all, "That's me; that's the way I am." But the Gita is addressing the true Self, the soul, cautioning the aspiring devotee against sympathy for that part of the nature that opposes the soul. It is good to feel good about the good in one's self; but it is bad to feel bad for the bad that should be destroyed.

continuance of life, O Govinda (Krishna)? The very ones for whose sake we desire empire, enjoyment, pleasure, remain poised here for battle, ready to relinquish wealth and life — preceptors, fathers, sons, grandfathers, uncles, fathers-in-law, grandsons, brothers-in-law, and other kinsmen. 32–34

Even though these relatives should try to destroy me, O Madhusudana (Krishna), still I could not want to destroy them, not even if thereby I attained mastery over the three worlds; how much less, then, for the sake of this mundane territory of earth!* 35

What happiness could we gain, O Janardana (Krishna), from destroying the clan of Dhritarashtra? The slaying of these felons would only put us in the clutches of sin. 36

Therefore, we are not justified in annihilating our very own relatives, the progeny of Dhritarashtra. O Madhava (Krishna), how indeed could we attain happiness by killing our own kindred? 37

Even if these others (the Kurus), whose understanding is eclipsed by greed, behold no calamity in the ruin of families, and no evil in enmity to friends, should we not know to avoid this sin, O Janardana (Krishna) — we who do distinctly perceive the evil in the disintegration of the family? 38–39

With the decimation of the family, the age-old religious rites of the family fade away. When the upholding religion is annihilated, then sin overpowers the whole family.† 40

O Krishna, from lack of religion the women of the family become bad. O Varshneya (Krishna), women being thus contaminated, adultery is engendered among castes. 41

---

* "The three worlds" refers to the triple cosmos: causal (mental), astral (energy), physical (matter). God created all matter mentally; then He manifested the causal ideas as an astral or energy universe; finally He precipitated the astral lifetrons into the forms of the visible universe....The physical world is in reality nothing more than inert matter. The inherent life and animation in all forms, from atoms to man, come from the subtle forces of the astral world. These, in turn, have evolved from the still finer forces of the causal or ideational creation, the creative vibratory thoughts emanating from the consciousness of God.

† "Family": the diverse instruments of consciousness and action in man, derived from their progenitors/"ancestors" of Cosmic Consciousness, soul consciousness, etc. *(Publisher's Note)*

The adulteration of family blood consigns to hell the clan-destroyers, along with the family itself. Their ancestors, by being denied the oblations of rice-ball and water, are degraded.   42

By these misdeeds of the family-destroyers, producing admixture of castes, the time-old rites (*dharmas*) of the caste and clan are annihilated.   43

O Janardana (Krishna), often have we heard that men devoid of family religious rites are most certainly committed to reside indefinitely in hell.*   44

Alas! actuated by greed for the comfort of possessing a kingdom, we are prepared to kill our own kinsmen — an act surely entangling us in great iniquity.   45

If, weapons in hand, the sons of Dhritarashtra kill me, wholly resigned and weaponless in the battle, that solution will be more welcome and beneficial to me!   46

Sanjaya said (to Dhritarashtra):

Arjuna, having spoken thus on the battlefield, his mind disturbed by grief, flinging away his bow and arrows, sat down on the seat of his chariot.   47

Aum, Tat, Sat.

In the Upanishad of the holy Bhagavad Gita — the discourse of Lord Krishna to Arjuna, which is the scripture of yoga and the science of God-realization — this is the first chapter, called "The Despondency of Arjuna on the Path of Yoga."

---

* *Narake* (in hell) *'niyataṁ* (*aniyataṁ,* "indefinitely") *vāso bhavatī* (to be or reside in a place or dwelling). An alternate Sanskrit reading supplies the word *niyataṁ* (certainly, inevitably) instead of *aniyataṁ.* Both possibilities have been combined in this translation.

CHAPTER II

Sankhya and Yoga: Cosmic Wisdom and the Method of Its Attainment

The Lord's Exhortation to the Devotee, and the Devotee's Plea for Guidance

Sanjaya said (to Dhritarashtra):

Madhusudana (Krishna) then addressed him whose eyes were bedimmed with tears, and who was overcome with pity and discouragement.　　　　　　　　　　　　　　　　　　　　1

The Lord said:

In such a critical moment, whence comes upon thee, O Arjuna, this despondency — behavior improper for an Aryan, disgraceful, detrimental to the attainment of heaven?　　　　　　　　　　2

O Partha ("Son of Pritha," Arjuna), surrender not to unmanliness; it is unbecoming to thee. O Scorcher of Foes, forsake this small weak-heartedness! Arise!　　　　　　　　　　　　　　　　3

Arjuna said:

O Slayer of Madhu, O Destroyer of Foes (Krishna)! how can I, in this war, direct arrows against Bhishma and Drona* — beings who should be worshiped!　　　　　　　　　　　　　　　4

Even a life of beggary would be more salutary for me than a life marred by slaying my high-souled preceptors! If I do destroy these mentors who are intent on wealth and possessions (the objects of the senses), then surely here on earth all my would-be enjoyment of material happiness will be dreadfully bloodstained!　　　5

I can hardly decide which end would be better — that they should conquer us? or that we should conquer them? Confronting us are

* Symbolically, one's ego and habit-inclinations (see pages 41 ff.).

Dhritarashtra's children — the very ones whose death would make our life undesirable!   6

With my inner nature overshadowed by weak sympathy and pity, with a mind in bewilderment about duty, I implore Thee to advise me what is the best path for me to follow. I am Thy disciple. Teach me, whose refuge is in Thee.   7

I behold nothing that will do away with this inner affliction that pounds my senses — nothing! not even my possession of an unrivaled and prosperous kingship over this earth and lordship over the deities of heaven!   8

Sanjaya said (to Dhritarashtra):

Having thus addressed Hrishikesha (Krishna), Gudakesha-Parantapa (Arjuna) declared to Govinda (Krishna): "I will not fight!"; then remained silent.   9

O Bharata (Dhritarashtra), to him who was lamenting between the two armies, the Lord of the Senses (Krishna), as if smiling, spoke in the following way: 10

The Eternal, Transcendental Nature of the Soul

The Blessed Lord said:

Thou hast been lamenting for those not worth thy lamentations! Yet thou dost utter words of lore. The truly wise mourn neither for those who are living nor for those who have passed away.   11

It is not that I have never before been incarnated; nor thou, nor these other royal ones! And never in all futurity shall any one of us not exist!   12

As in the body the embodied Self passes through childhood, youth, and old age, so is its passage into another body; the wise thereat are not disturbed.   13

O Son of Kunti (Arjuna), the ideas of heat and cold, pleasure and pain, are produced by the contacts of the senses with their objects. Such ideas are limited by a beginning and an end. They are transitory, O

Descendant of Bharata (Arjuna); bear them with patience!   14

O Flower among Men (Arjuna)! he who cannot be ruffled by these (contacts of the senses with their objects), who is calm and evenminded during pain and pleasure, he alone is fit to attain everlastingness!   15

Of the unreal, there is no existence. Of the real, there is no nonexistence. The final truth of both of these is known by men of wisdom.   16

Know as imperishable the One by whom everything has been manifested and pervaded. No one has power to bring about the annihilation of this Unchangeable Spirit.   17

Regarded as having a termination of existence are these fleshly garments; immutable, imperishable, and limitless is the Indwelling Self. With this wisdom, O Descendant of Bharata (Arjuna), battle thou!   18

He who considers the Self as the slayer; he who deems that it can be slain: neither of these knows the truth. The Self does not kill, nor is it killed.   19

This Self is never born nor does it ever perish; nor having come into existence will it again cease to be. It is birthless, eternal, changeless, eversame (unaffected by the usual processes associated with time). It is not slain when the body is killed.   20

How can he who knows the Self to be imperishable, everlastingly permanent, birthless and changeless, possibly think that this Self can cause the destruction of another? O Partha (Arjuna), whom does it slay?*   21

Just as an individual forsaking dilapidated raiment dons new clothes, so the body-encased soul, relinquishing decayed bodily habitations, enters others that are new.   22

No weapon can pierce the soul; no fire can burn it; no water can moisten it; nor can any wind wither it.   23

The soul is uncleavable; it cannot be burnt or wetted or dried. The

---

*[In addition to its literal meaning, pointing out the immortality of the soul], this stanza conveys also a deep metaphysical lesson....Even if you destroy the wicked attachments of the senses, you are foolish to think that the senses themselves will be destroyed! Your higher Self only purifies the lower self; It does not destroy it.

soul is immutable, all-permeating, ever calm, and immovable — eternally the same.   24

The soul is said to be imponderable, unmanifested, and unchangeable. Therefore, knowing it to be such, thou shouldst not lament!   25

But if thou dost imagine this soul incessantly to be born and to die, even in that case, O Mighty-armed (Arjuna), thou shouldst not grieve for it. For that which is born must die, and that which is dead must be born again. Why then shouldst thou grieve about the unavoidable?   26–27

The beginning of all creatures is veiled, the middle is manifested, and the end again is imperceptible, O Bharata (Arjuna). Why, then, lament this truth?   28

Some behold the soul in amazement. Similarly, others describe it as marvelous. Still others listen about the soul as wondrous. And there are others who, even after hearing all about the soul, do not comprehend it at all.   29

Symbolic Meaning of Verse 30:

On the metaphysical plane of interpretation, as relates to the inner spiritual battle of the devotee-Arjuna, an important point is made in this and preceding verses about the inviolability of the soul. The Lord reminds the aspirant of his innate soul-power to become victorious over his lower ego-nature. Devotees who are addicted to the weakness of their senses and bad habits are not only reluctant to destroy these friendly enemies, but also feel that the overwhelming power of these forces shall surely succeed in the genocide of the soul's divine qualities and aspirations. But though ego, habit, senses, desires, may enshroud man's consciousness for a while, they cannot destroy nor change the soul, nor suppress it forever. Every soul, no matter how "dead" it seems, nor how deeply buried beneath bad habits of ego consciousness, is able to resurrect itself from the sepulchre of wickedness and prenatal and postnatal weaknesses. The soul is indestructible, and untouched and unchanged by its would-be enemies; it only awaits the rallying call of the determined divine warrior.

O Bharata (Arjuna), the One who dwells in the bodies of all is eternally inviolable. Grieve not, therefore, for any created being.   30

The Righteous Battle Is Man's Religious Duty

Even from the point of view of thine own *dharma* (one's rightful duty) thou shouldst not inwardly oscillate! There is nothing more propitious for a *Kshatriya* than a righteous battle.   31

O son of Pritha (Arjuna), fortunate are the *Kshatriyas* when such a righteous battle has, unprovoked, fallen to their lot; they find therein an open door to heaven.   32

But if thou declinest to undertake this righteous combat, then, having relinquished thine own *dharma* and glory, thou wilt reap sin.   33

Men will ever speak of thine ignominy. To the man of repute, dishonor is veritably worse than death.   34

The mighty chariot warriors will assume that thou hast shunned this war through fear. Thus wilt thou be lightly regarded by those who had thought highly of thee.   35

Thy foes will speak contemptuously (words improper to utter), maligning thy powers. What could be more painful than this?   36

If thou shouldst die (battling thine enemies), thou wilt gain heaven; if thou conquerest, thou wilt enjoy the earth. Therefore, O son of Kunti (Arjuna), lift thyself up! Be determined to fight!   37

Equalizing (by evenmindedness) happiness and sorrow, profit and loss, triumph and failure — so encounter thou the battle! Thus thou wilt not acquire sin.   38

Yoga: Remedy for Doubt, Confusion, and Intellectual Dissatisfaction

The ultimate wisdom of Sankhya I have explained to thee. But now thou must hear about the wisdom of Yoga, equipped with which, O Partha (Arjuna), thou shalt shatter the bonds of karma.   39

In this path (of yoga action) there is no loss of the unfinished effort for realization, nor is there creation of contrary effects. Even a tiny bit of this real religion protects one from great fear (the colossal sufferings inherent in the repeated cycles of birth and death).   40

In this Yoga, O Scion of Kuru* (Arjuna), the inner determination is single, one-pointed; whereas the reasonings of the undecided mind are unending and variously ramified.   41

O Partha (Arjuna), no single-pointed resolution (no fixity of mind) in the meditative state of *samadhi* grows in those who cling tenaciously to power and sense delights, and whose discriminative intelligence is led astray by the flowery declamations of the spiritually ignorant. Contending that there is naught else than to rejoice in the laudatory aphorisms of the Vedas, their true nature being afflicted with earthly inclinations, having heaven (the pleasurable phenomena of the astral world) as their highest goal, performing the numerous specific sacrificial rites for the purpose of obtaining enjoyment and power — such persons embrace instead the cause of new births, the consequences of these (desire-instigated) actions.   42–44

The Vedas are concerned with the three universal qualities or *gunas*. O Arjuna, free thyself from the triple qualities and from the pairs of opposites! Ever calm, harboring no thoughts of receiving and keeping, become thou settled in the Self.   45

To the knower of Brahman (Spirit), all the Vedas (scriptures) are of no more utility than is a reservoir when there is a flood from all directions.   46

The Yoga Art of Right Action That Leads to Infinite Wisdom

Thy human right is for activity only, never for the resultant fruit of actions. Do not consider thyself the creator of the fruits of thy activities; neither allow thyself attachment to inactivity.   47

---

* Kuru was an ancestor of both the Pandavas and the Kauravas, thus Arjuna is here referred to as Kurunandana, descendant of Kuru; *nandana* also has the connotation of something that causes rejoicing — thus Krishna encourages Arjuna by addressing him as "the pride or choice son of the Kuru dynasty."

O Dhananjaya (Arjuna), remaining immersed in yoga, perform all actions, forsaking attachment (to their fruits), being indifferent to success and failure. This mental evenness is termed yoga. 48

Ordinary action (performed with desire) is greatly inferior to action united to the guidance of wisdom; therefore, O Dhananjaya (Arjuna), seek shelter in the ever-directing wisdom. Miserable are those who perform actions only for their fruits. 49

One who is united to cosmic wisdom goes beyond the effects of both virtue and vice, even here in this life. Therefore, devote thyself to yoga, divine union. Yoga is the art of proper action. 50

Those who have mastered their minds become engrossed in infinite wisdom; they have no further interest in any fruits of actions. Freed thus from the chain of rebirth, they attain the state beyond sorrow. 51

When thine intelligence penetrates beyond the darkness of delusion, then wilt thou attain indifference regarding matters that have been heard and matters yet to be heard. 52

When thine intelligence, bewildered by the variety of revealed

Outer Rites Versus Self-realization

"The Vedas praise and worship the activating forces of Nature that spume her many forms from the roil of the trifold qualities [the *gunas*]. But, O devotee, concentrate your attention not on matter but on Spirit, and thus free yourself from emotional involvement in Nature's dream pictures of good, active, and evil existence. Ever adherent to your true nature (*nityasattvastha*) — quiescent, undisturbed by the triadic qualities and their light-and-shadow pairs of opposites — free from the delusion-woven nets of desires and attachments, become permanently established in your transcendent Self."

This stanza [II:45] points out the spiritual inefficacy of the practice, however perfect and austere, of the merely external rites mentioned in the scriptures. Nothing but the cleansing of man's inward being has the power to free him from the trifold reincarnation-making qualities of human nature — the sattvic (elevating), the rajasic (activating), and the tamasic (degrading).

truths, becomes securely anchored in the ecstasy of soul bliss, then wilt thou attain the final union (yoga).   53

Qualities of the Self-Realized

Arjuna said:

O Keshava (Krishna)! what are the characteristics of the sage who possesses ever calm wisdom and who is steeped in *samadhi* (ecstasy)? How does this man of steady wisdom speak and sit and walk?   54

The Blessed Lord replied:

O Partha (Arjuna)! when a man completely relinquishes all desires of the mind, and is entirely contented in the Self, by the Self, he is then considered to be one settled in wisdom.   55

He whose consciousness is not shaken by anxiety under afflictions nor by attachment to happiness under favorable circumstances; he who is free from worldly loves, fears, and angers — he is called a *muni* of steady discrimination.   56

He who is everywhere nonattached, neither joyously excited by encountering good nor disturbed by evil, has an established wisdom.   57

When the yogi, like a tortoise withdrawing its limbs, can fully retire his senses from the objects of perception, his wisdom manifests steadiness.   58

The man who physically fasts from sense objects finds that the sense objects fall away for a little while, leaving behind only the longing for them. But he who beholds the Supreme is freed even from longings.   59

O son of Kunti (Arjuna), the eager excitable senses do forcibly seize the consciousness even of one who has a high degree of enlightenment, and is striving (for liberation).   60

He who unites his spirit to Me, having subjugated all his senses, remains concentrated on Me as the Supremely Desirable. The intuitive wisdom of that yogi becomes steadfast whose senses are under his sway.   61

Brooding on sense objects causes attachment to them. Attachment breeds craving; craving breeds anger. Anger breeds delusion; delusion breeds loss of memory (of the Self). Loss of right memory causes decay of the discriminating faculty. From decay of discrimination, annihilation (of spiritual life) follows.   62–63

The man of self-control, roaming among material objects with subjugated senses, and devoid of attraction and repulsion, attains an unshakable inner calmness.   64

In soul bliss* all grief is annihilated. Indeed, the discrimination of the blissful man soon becomes firmly established (in the Self).   65

To the disunited (one not established in the Self) does not belong wisdom, nor has he meditation. To the unmeditative there is no tranquility. To the peaceless how comes happiness?   66

As a boat on the waters is carried off course by a gale, so an individual's discrimination is driven from its intended path when the mind succumbs to the wandering senses.   67

O Mighty-armed (Arjuna), his wisdom is well-established whose sense faculties are wholly subjugated in regard to sense objects.   68

That which is night (of slumber) to all creatures is (luminous) wakefulness to the man of self-mastery. And what is wakefulness to ordinary men, that is night (a time for slumber) to the divinely perceptive sage.   69

He is full with contentment who absorbs all desires within, as the brimful ocean remains unmoved (unchanged) by waters entering into it — not he who lusts after desires.   70

That person realizes peace who, relinquishing all desires, exists without craving and is unidentified with the mortal ego and its sense of "mine-ness."   71

O Partha (Arjuna)! this is the "established in Brahman" state. Anyone entering this state is never (again) deluded. Even at the very moment of transition (from the physical to the astral), if one be-

---

* "In soul bliss," *prasāde:* "In the all-satisfying state of inner calmness (i.e., that perfect tranquility of the Self that is permeated with the soul's pure nature, ever new bliss)."

comes anchored therein, he attains the final, irrevocable, state of
Spirit-communion.   72

Aum, Tat, Sat.

*In the Upanishad of the holy Bhagavad Gita — the discourse of Lord
Krishna to Arjuna, which is the scripture of yoga and the science of
God-realization — this is the second chapter, called "Sankhya-Yoga."*

Brahmasthiti: Liberation From the Three Worlds of Finite Creation

Enthronement in the omnipresent consciousness of Spirit ["established in
Brahman"] is spoken of as *Brahmasthiti,* the state of reigning in the Royal Spirit.
The Spirit-reigning yogi, freed while living, is never again deluded, nor does he
come down to a lesser state. He lives in the consciousness of God. His soul ex-
pands into the Spirit, yet he retains his individuality, immersed everlastingly in
Spirit-communion.

❖ ❖ ❖

In the transcendental state God spins out His dreams of ideational (causal), astral, and physical universes. The physical cosmos, with its many "island universes"
floating in the eternal void, is encircled by a nimbus of radiant energy that melts
away into the larger astral world. The astral cosmos is a grander manifestation of
creation than the physical, and runs through and beyond the latter....The causal universe is the womb of creation. In the causal universe, God's finest creative forces
of consciousness, and highly evolved beings with their intuitive processes, objec-
tify universes from subtle divine thought forces....

The yogi who has attained complete control over his consciousness can behold
the physical, astral, or causal worlds, or go beyond to the transcendent vibration-
less region of God.

❖ ❖ ❖

When the yogi is established in the Ethereal Infinitude, even if attained only at the
moment when the soul slips from the physical tenement into the astral, that soul enters *Brahmanirvana,* expansion in Spirit through the extinguishment of ego and all
desires that compel a soul to reincarnate. An omnipresent being cannot be caged
behind the bars of finite incarnations. He can of his own free will retain a physical
or an astral body, but it cannot imprison his overarching spirit.

Karma Yoga: The Path of Spiritual Action

Why Is Activity a Necessary Part of the Path to Liberation?

Arjuna said:

O Janardana (Krishna)! if thou dost consider understanding to be superior to action, why then, O Keshava (Krishna), dost thou enjoin on me this awful activity?   1

With these apparently conflicting speeches thou art, as it were, confusing my intelligence. Please let me know for certain that one thing by which I will achieve the highest good.   2

The Cosmic Lord said:

O Sinless One, at the onset of creation, a twofold way of salvation was given by Me to this world: for the wise, divine union through wisdom; for the yogis, divine union through active meditation.   3

Actionlessness is not attained simply by avoiding actions. By forsaking work no one reaches perfection.   4

Verily, no one can stay for even a moment without working; all are indeed compelled to perform actions willy-nilly, prodded by the qualities (*gunas*) born of Nature (Prakriti).   5

The individual who forcibly controls the organs of action, but whose mind rotates around thoughts of sense objects, is said to be a hypocrite, deluding himself.   6

But that man succeeds supremely, O Arjuna, who, disciplining the senses by the mind, unattached, keeps his organs of activity steadfast on the path of God-uniting actions.   7

Perform thou those actions that are obligatory, for action is better than inactivity; even simple maintenance of thy body would be impossible through inaction.   8

The Nature of Right Action: Performing All Works as Oblations (Yajna)

Worldly people are karmically bound by activities that differ from those performed as *yajna* (religious rites); O Son of Kunti (Arjuna), labor thou, nonattached, in the spirit of *yajna*, offering actions as oblations.   9

Prajapati (Brahma as the Creator of *praja* or human beings), having made mankind in the beginning, along with *Yajna*, said: "By this shalt thou propagate; this will be the milch cow of thy longings. With this *yajna*, meditate on the *devas*,* and may those *devas* think of thee; thus communing with one another, thou shalt receive the Supreme Good. The *devas* communed with by *yajna* will grant thee the craved-for gifts of life." He who enjoys benefactions of the universal deities without due offerings to them is indeed a thief.   10–12

Saints — those who eat the remnants of due fire offerings (*yajna*) — are freed from all sin; but sinners — those who make food just for themselves — feast on sin.   13

From food, creatures spring forth; from rain, food is begotten. From *Yajna* (the sacrificial cosmic fire), rain issues forth; the cosmic fire (cosmic light) is born of karma (divine vibratory action).   14

Know this divine vibratory activity to have come into being from Brahma (God's Creative Consciousness); and this Creative Consciousness to derive from the Imperishable (the Everlasting Spirit). Therefore, God's Creative Consciousness (Brahma), which is all-pervading, is inherently and inseparably present in *Yajna* (the cosmic fire or light, which in turn is the essence of all components of vibratory creation).   15

That man, O Son of Pritha (Arjuna), who in this world does not follow the wheel thus set rotating, living in iniquity and contented in the senses, lives in vain!   16

But the individual who truly loves the soul and is fully satisfied

---

* *Devas:* astral deities; literally, "shining ones" — the divine or angelic forces that uphold the material world. (*Publisher's Note*)

with the soul and finds utter contentment in the soul alone, for him
no duty exists.   17

Such a person has no purpose of gain in this world by performing
actions, nor does he lose anything by their nonperformance. He is not
dependent on anyone for anything.   18

True Meaning of Yajna, Sacrificial Fire Rite

Worldly people perform actions with selfish motives and the desire to gain material profit and happiness. Owing to that inclination, they are karmically tied to the earth throughout successive incarnations.

The yogi, however, strives to perform good actions in a spirit of selflessness and nonattachment; he thereby quickens his evolution toward soul freedom. All such liberating divine duties may be termed *yajna*....

The formal rite [*yajna*] in India of pouring into a fire clarified butter (ghee) —a form of fire-purified matter—is symbolical of uniting life energy with cosmic energy.

The initiate in guru-given yoga meditation performs the *esoteric* real fire rite enjoined by the Hindu scriptures. He withdraws his life force from the sensory and motor nerves and pours that energy into the sacred fires of life gathered in the seven occult cerebrospinal centers.

When the yogi switches off the life current from the nerves, he finds his mind disconnected from the senses. This act of withdrawing life from the body and uniting that energy with the light of God [*Kriya Yoga*] is the highest *yajna,* the real fire rite—casting the little flame of life into the Great Divine Fire, burning all human desire in the divine desire for God. Then the yogi takes his sense-withdrawn mind and casts it into the fire of Cosmic Consciousness; realizing, finally, his own soul as something entirely different from the body, he casts that Self into the fire of Eternal Spirit.

The true *exoteric* fire rite of life—by which the bodily life is united with the Cosmic Life, and the human mind and soul are united with the Cosmic Mind and Spirit—consists in offering right actions to God, without desire or attachment.

These followers of right actions performed as *yajna* do not remain tied to the earth, but are liberated.

Righteous Duty, Performed With Nonattachment,
Is Godly

Therefore, always conscientiously perform good material actions (*karyam*) and spiritual actions (*karman*) without attachment. By doing all actions without attachment, one attains the highest.*   19

By the path of right action alone, Janaka and others like him reached perfection. Also, simply for the purpose of rightly guiding mortals, thou shouldst perform action.   20

Whatever a superior being does, inferior persons imitate. His actions set a standard for people of the world.   21

O Son of Pritha (Arjuna), no compelling duty have I to perform; there is naught that I have not acquired; nothing in the three worlds remains for Me to gain! Yet I am consciously present in the performance of all actions.   22

O Partha (Arjuna), if at any time I did not continue to perform actions, without pause, men would wholly imitate My way.   23

If I did not perform actions (in a balanced way), these universes would be annihilated. I would be the cause of dire confusion ("the improper admixture of duties"). I would thus be the instrument of men's ruination.   24

O Descendant of Bharata (Arjuna), as the ignorant perform actions with attachment and hope of reward, so the wise should act with dispassionate nonattachment, to serve gladly as a guide for the multitudes.   25

Under no circumstances should the wise disturb the understanding of ignorant persons who are attached to actions. Instead, the illumined being, by conscientiously performing activities, should inspire in the ignorant a desire for all dutiful actions.   26

---

* *Karma,* from the root *kri,* "to do," has the general meaning of "action." It can also mean, specifically, material action or dutiful action; religious rite or spiritual action—as also, the effects one reaps from his actions. The variants of the word *karma* have also interchangeable meanings, the intent determined by the context. Thus, in this verse, *karyam* refers to "dutiful material action" and *karman* denotes "religious rite, or spiritual action (i.e., meditative action)." *(Publisher's Note)*

How Egoless Action Frees the Yogi From Nature's Dualities and the Bondage of Karma

All action is universally engendered by the attributes (*gunas*) of primordial Nature (Prakriti). A man whose Self is deluded by egoity thinks, "I am the doer."   27

O Mighty-armed (Arjuna)! the knower of truth about the divisions of the *gunas* (attributes of Nature) and their actions — realizing it is the *gunas* as sense attributes that are attached to the *gunas* as sense objects — keeps (his Self) unattached to them.   28

The yogi of perfect wisdom should not bewilder the minds of men who have imperfect understanding. Deluded by the attributes of primordial Nature, the ignorant must cling to the activities engendered by those *gunas*.   29

Relinquish all activities unto Me! Devoid of egotism and expectation, with your attention concentrated on the soul, free from feverish worry, be engaged in the battle (of activity).   30

Right Attitude Toward One's Spiritual Guide and Sadhana

Men, devotion-filled, who ceaselessly practice My precepts, without fault-finding, they too become free from all karma.   31

But those who denounce this teaching of Mine and do not live according to it, wholly deluded in regard to true wisdom, know them, devoid of understanding, to be doomed.   32

Even the wise man acts according to the tendencies of his own nature. All living creatures go according to Nature; what can (superficial) suppression avail?   33

Attachment and repulsion of the senses for their specific objects are Nature-ordained. Beware the influence of this duality. Verily, these two (psychological qualities) are one's enemies!   34

One's own duty (*svadharma*), though deficient in quality, is superior to duty other than one's own (*paradharma*), though well accomplished.

Better it is to die in *svadharma; paradharma* is fraught with fear and
danger.   35

Conquering the Two-Sided Passion, Desire and Anger

Arjuna said:

O Varshneya (Krishna), by what is man impelled, even against his
will, to perform evil — compelled, it seems, by force?   36

The Blessed Lord said:

Born of the activating attribute of Nature (*rajo-guna*), it is desire,
it is anger, (that is the impelling force) — full of unappeasable craving
and great evil: know this (two-sided passion) to be the foulest enemy
here on earth.   37

As fire is obscured by smoke, as a looking glass by dust, as an embryo
is enveloped by the womb, so it (wisdom) is covered by this (desire).   38

O Son of Kunti (Arjuna)! the constant enemy of wise men is the
unslakable flame of desire, by which wisdom is concealed.   39

Desire and Anger: Duryodhana and His Evil Brother

Desire that is frustrated results in anger.* Thus the first son of the blind sense-
mind King Dhritarashtra is Duryodhana–Material Desire, and his second son
(closest brother to Duryodhana) is Duhshasana, symbolizing anger. The name
means, "hard to restrain or control," from the Sanskrit *duḥ,* "difficult"; and
śās, "to restrain or control."

In the *Mahabharata,* the altogether despicable Duhshasana well character-
izes the evil of anger. In the second chapter of the Gita, Krishna explains to Arjuna that anger causes the wrongdoer to be enveloped in delusion, which then
obscures memory of the correct behavior of the Self, causing decay of the discriminative faculty. From this confusion of intelligence, annihilation of right
behavior follows.

* *Krodha,* one of the six faults of the materialistic ego, as mentioned on page 41.

The senses, mind, and intellect are said to be desire's formidable stronghold; through these, desire deludes the embodied soul by eclipsing its wisdom. 40

Therefore, O Best of the Bharata Dynasty (Arjuna)! first discipline the senses, then destroy desire, the sinful annihilator of wisdom and Self-realization. 41

The senses are said to be superior (to the physical body); the mind is superior to the sense faculties; the intelligence is superior to the mind; but he (the Self) is superior to the intelligence. 42

O Mighty-armed (Arjuna)! thus cognizing the Self as superior to the intelligence, and disciplining the self (ego) by the Self (soul), annihilate the foe! hard-to-conquer, wearing the form of desire. 43

Aum, Tat, Sat.

In the Upanishad of the holy Bhagavad Gita — the discourse of Lord Krishna to Arjuna, which is the scripture of yoga and the science of God-realization — this is the third chapter, called "Karma Yoga."

CHAPTER IV

The Supreme Science of Knowing God

The Historical Basis and Esoteric Essence of Yoga

The exalted Lord said (to Arjuna):

I gave this imperishable Yoga to Vivasvat (the sun-god); Vivasvat passed on the knowledge to Manu (the Hindu lawgiver); Manu told it to Ikshvaku (founder of the solar dynasty of the *Kshatriyas*). Handed down in this way in orderly succession, the *Rajarishis* (royal *rishis*) knew it. But, O Scorcher of Foes (Arjuna)! by the long passage of time, this Yoga was lost sight of on earth.*   1–2

I have this day informed thee about that same ancient yoga, for thou art My devotee and friend. This sacred mystery (of yoga) is, indeed, the producer of supreme benefit (to mankind).   3

Arjuna said:

Vivasvat was born first, and thy birth occurred later. How then can I comprehend thy words that thou didst communicate this yoga in the beginning (before thy birth)?   4

The Blessed Lord said:

O Arjuna, many births have been experienced by Me and by thee. I am acquainted with them all, whereas thou rememberest them not, O Scorcher of Foes.   5

Unborn though I am, of changeless Essence! yet becoming Lord of all creation, abiding in My own Cosmic Nature (Prakriti), I embody Myself by Self-evolved *maya*-delusion.   6

---

* These two verses proclaim the historical antiquity of *Raja* ("royal") *Yoga*, the eternal, immutable science of uniting soul and Spirit. At the same time, understood esoterically, they give a concise description of that science—the steps by which the soul descends from Cosmic Consciousness to the mortal state of identification with the human body, and the route it must take to reascend to its Source, the all-blissful Eternal Spirit. [See commentary in *God Talks With Arjuna*.]

O Bharata (Arjuna)! whenever virtue (*dharma*) declines and vice (*adharma*) predominates, I incarnate as an Avatar. In visible form I appear from age to age to protect the virtuous and to destroy evildoing in order to reestablish righteousness.   7–8

Paths of Liberation From the Rounds of Rebirth

He who thus intuits, in their reality of orderly principles, My divine manifestations and vibratory actions, is not reborn after death; he obtains Me, O Arjuna!   9

Sanctified by the asceticism of wisdom, disengaged from attachment, fear, and ire, engrossed and sheltered in Me, many beings have attained My nature.   10

O Partha (Arjuna)! in whatever way people are devoted to Me, in that measure I manifest Myself to them. All men, in every manner (of seeking Me), pursue a path to Me.   11

Desiring success of their actions here on earth, men adore the gods (various ideals), because achievement accruing from activity is readily attained in the world of men.   12

According to the differentiation of attributes (*gunas*) and actions (*karma*), I have created the four castes. Though thus the Doer, yet know Me to be the Nonperformer, beyond all change.   13

Actions do not cause attachment in Me, nor have I longings for their fruits. He who is identified with Me, who knows My nature, is also free from the karmic fetters of works.   14

Understanding this, wise men who have sought after salvation, since pristine times, have performed dutiful actions. Therefore, do thou also act dutifully, even as did the ancients of bygone ages.   15

Freedom From Karma: The Nature of Right Action, Wrong Action, and Inaction

Even the wise are confused about action and inaction. Therefore I will explain what constitutes true action — a knowledge that will free thee from evil.   16

The nature of karma (action) is very difficult to know. Verily, in order to understand fully the nature of proper action, one has also to understand the nature of contrary (wrong) action and the nature of inaction.   17

He is a yogi, discriminative among men, who beholds inactivity in action and action in inaction. He has attained the goal of all actions (and is free).   18

The sages call that man wise whose pursuits are all without self-ish plan or longings for results, and whose activities are purified (cauterized of karmic outgrowths) by the fire of wisdom.   19

Relinquishing attachment to the fruits of work, always contented, independent (of material rewards), the wise do not perform any (binding) action even in the midst of activities.   20

He incurs no evil performing mere bodily actions who has re-nounced all sense of possession, who is free from (delusive human) hopes, and whose heart (the power of feeling) is controlled by the soul.*   21

That man of action is free from karma who receives with content-ment whate'er befalls him, who is poised above the dualities, who is devoid of jealousy or envy or enmity, and who looks equally on gain and loss.   22

Yajna, the Spiritual Fire Rite That Consumes All Karma

All karma, or effects of actions, completely melts away from the liberated being who, free from attachments, with his mind enveloped in wisdom, performs the true spiritual fire rite (*yajna*).†   23

The process of offering and the oblation itself — both are Spirit. The fire and he who makes oblation into it are other forms of Spirit. By realizing this, being absorbed in Brahman (Spirit) during all activi-ties, verily such a one goes to Spirit alone.   24

---

* *Yata-citta-ātmā:* lit., "his soul having controlled his heart (*chitta*)." *Chitta* is a comprehensive term for the aggregate of mind-stuff that produces intelligent consciousness, the power of feeling.

† Lit., *yajñāya,* "for the purpose of sacrificial worship"; *ācaratas,* "casting into the fire."

In truth, there are those yogis who sacrifice to *devas;* others offer the self, as a sacrifice made by the self, in the fire of Spirit alone.   25

Certain devotees offer, as oblations in the fire of inner control, their powers of hearing and other senses. Others offer as sacrifice, in the fire of the senses, sound and other sense objects.   26

Again, others (followers of the path of *Jnana Yoga*) offer all their sense activities and the functions of the life force as oblations in the wisdom-kindled yoga flame of inner control in Self.   27

Other devotees offer as oblations wealth, self-discipline, and the methods of Yoga; while other individuals, self-controlled and keeping strict vows, offer as sacrifices the study of self and the acquirement of scriptural wisdom.   28

Other devotees offer as sacrifice the incoming breath of *prana* in the outgoing breath of *apana,* and the outgoing breath of *apana* in the incoming breath of *prana,* thus arresting the cause of inhalation and exhalation (rendering breath unnecessary) by intent practice of *pranayama* (the life-control technique of *Kriya Yoga*).*   29

Other devotees, by a scheme of proper diet, offer all the different kinds of *prana* and their functions as oblations in the fire of the one common *prana.*

All such devotees (adepts in all the foregoing *yajnas*) are knowers of the true fire ceremony (of wisdom) that consumes their karmic sins.   30

By partaking of the nectar-remnant of any of these spiritual fire ceremonies, they (the yogis) go to the Infinite Spirit (Brahman). But this realization of Spirit belongs not to ordinary men of this world who are nonperformers of the true spiritual rites. Without real sacrifice, O Flower of the Kurus (Arjuna), whence comes any better world (any better existence or elevated state of consciousness)?   31

Various spiritual ceremonies (*yajnas* performed with wisdom or with material objects) are thus found in the wisdom-temple of the Vedas ("mouth of Brahman"). Know them all to be the offsprings of

---

* Explained further in sidebar accompanying V:27–28, page 92.

action; and understanding this (and by the performance of those actions), thou shalt find salvation.   32

The spiritual fire ceremony of wisdom, O Scorcher of Foes (Arjuna)!
is superior to any material ritual. All action in its entirety (the act, the
cause, the karmic effect) is consummated in wisdom.   33

The All-Sanctifying Wisdom, Imparted by a True Guru

Understand this! By surrendering thyself (to the guru), by ques-
tioning (the guru and thine inner perception), and by service (to the
guru), the sages who have realized truth will impart that wisdom to
thee.   34

Comprehending that wisdom from a guru, thou, O Pandava
(Arjuna)! wilt not again fall into delusion; for by that wisdom thou
shalt behold the entire creation in thyself, and then in Me (Spirit).   35

Even if thou art the chief sinner among all sinners, yet by the sole
raft of wisdom thou shalt safely cross the sea of sin.   36

O Arjuna, as enkindled flame converts firewood into ashes, so does
the fire of wisdom consume to ashes all karma.   37

Verily, nothing else in this world is as sanctifying as wisdom. In
due course of time, the devotee who is successful in yoga will sponta-

---

Who Can Serve as a Guru?

The *Guru Gita* (verse 17) aptly describes the guru as "dispeller of darkness"
(from *gu,* "darkness," and *ru,* "that which dispels"). Though today the word *guru*
is commonly used to refer simply to a teacher or instructor, a true guru is one who
is God-illumined. In his attainment of self-mastery, he has realized his identity with
the omnipresent Spirit. Such a one is uniquely qualified to lead the seeker on his
or her spiritual journey toward enlightenment and liberation.

"To keep company with the guru," wrote Swami Sri Yukteswar in *The Holy Science,* "is not only to be in his physical presence (as this is sometimes impossible),
but mainly means to keep him in our hearts and to be one with him in principle
and to attune ourselves with him."

neously realize this within his Self. 38

The man of devotion who is engrossed in the Infinite, who has controlled the senses, achieves wisdom. Having obtained wisdom, he immediately attains supreme peace. 39

The ignorant, the man lacking in devotion, the doubt-filled man, ultimately perishes. The unsettled individual has neither this world (earthly happiness), nor the next (astral happiness), nor the supreme happiness of God. 40

O Winner of Wealth (Arjuna), he who has relinquished work by yoga, and who has torn apart his doubts by wisdom, becomes poised in the Self; actions do not entangle him. 41

Therefore, O Descendant of Bharata (Arjuna), arise! Take shelter in yoga, slashing with the sword of wisdom this ignorance-born doubt existing in thy heart about the Self! 42

Aum, Tat, Sat.

In the Upanishad of the holy Bhagavad Gita — the discourse of Lord Krishna to Arjuna, which is the scripture of yoga and the science of God-realization — this is the fourth chapter, called "Jnana Yoga (Union Through Knowledge of the Divine)."

CHAPTER V

Freedom Through Inner Renunciation

Which Is Better: Serving in the World
or Seeking Wisdom in Seclusion?

Arjuna said:

O Krishna, you speak of renunciation of actions; at the same time, you advise their performance. Of these two, which is the better path? Please tell me for certain.   1

The Blessed Lord answered:

Salvation is found by both renunciation and performance of action. But of these two, the Yoga of works is better than renunciation of works.   2

O Mighty-armed (Arjuna), he is to be known as a constant *sannyasi* (renunciant), easily liberated from all entanglements, who has neither likes nor dislikes because he is unbound by the dualities (Nature's pairs of opposites).   3

Not sages but children speak of differences between the path of wisdom (Sankhya) and the path of spiritual activity (Yoga). He who is truly established in either one receives the fruits of both.   4

The state attained by the wise (the *jnana yogis* who successfully follow the wisdom path of discrimination — Sankhya) is also attained by the doers (the *karma yogis* who succeed through the performance of the scientific methods of yoga). He has truth who beholds as one both wisdom and right action.*   5

---

* See explanation of esoteric and exoteric meanings of *jnana* and *karma yoga*, page 53.

The Gita's Way of Freedom: Meditation on God Plus Desireless Activity

But renunciation, O Mighty-armed (Arjuna)! is difficult to achieve without God-uniting actions (yoga). By the practice of yoga, the *muni* ("he whose mind is absorbed in God") quickly attains the Infinite.   6

No taint (karmic involvement) touches the sanctified man of action who is engaged in divine communion (yoga), who has conquered ego consciousness (by attaining soul perception), who is victorious over his senses, and who feels his self as the Self existing in all beings.   7

The cognizer of truth, united to God, automatically perceives, "I myself do nothing" — even though he sees, hears, touches, smells, eats, moves, sleeps, breathes, speaks, rejects, holds, opens or closes his eyes — realizing that it is the senses (activated by Nature) that work amid sense objects.   8–9

Like unto the lotus leaf that remains unsullied by water, the yogi who performs actions, forswearing attachment and surrendering his actions to the Infinite, remains unbound by entanglement in the senses.   10

For sanctification of the ego, yogis perform actions solely with (the instruments of action) the body, the mind, discrimination, or even the senses, forsaking attachment (disallowing ego involvement, with its attachments and desires).   11

The God-united yogi, abandoning attachment to fruits of actions, attains the peace unshakable (peace born of self-discipline). The man who is not united to God is ruled by desires; through such attachment he remains in bondage.   12

The Self as Transcendental Witness: Ensconced in Bliss, Unaffected by the World

The embodied soul, controller of the senses, having mentally relinquished all activities, remains blissfully in the bodily city of nine gates — neither performing actions himself nor making others (the senses) perform actions.   13

The Lord God does not create in men the consciousness of being doers of actions, nor does He cause actions by them, nor does He entangle them with the fruits of actions. Delusive Cosmic Nature is the originator of all these.   14

The All-Pervading takes no account of anyone's virtue or sin. Wisdom is eclipsed by cosmic delusion; mankind is thereby bewildered.   15

But in those who have banished ignorance by Self-knowledge, their wisdom, like the illuminating sun, makes manifest the Supreme Self.   16

Their thoughts immersed in That (Spirit), their souls one with Spirit, their sole allegiance and devotion given to Spirit, their beings purified from poisonous delusion by the antidote of wisdom — such men reach the state of nonreturn.   17

Self-realized sages behold with an equal eye a learned and humble Brahmin, a cow, an elephant, a dog, and an outcaste.   18

The relativities of existence (birth and death, pleasure and pain) have been overcome, even here in this world, by those of fixed equal-mindedness. Thereby are they enthroned in Spirit — verily, the taintless, the perfectly balanced Spirit.   19

The knower of Spirit, abiding in the Supreme Being, with unswerving discrimination, free from delusion, is thus neither jubilant at pleasant experiences nor downcast by unpleasant experiences.   20

Transcending the Sensory World, Attaining the Bliss Indestructible

Unattracted to the sensory world, the yogi experiences the ever new joy inherent in the Self. Engaged in divine union of the soul with Spirit, he attains bliss indestructible.   21

O Son of Kunti (Arjuna)! because sense pleasures spring from outward contacts, and have beginning and end (are ephemeral), they are begetters only of misery. No sage seeks happiness from them.   22

He is truly a yogi who, on this earth and up to the very time of death, is able to master every impulse of desire and wrath. He is a happy man! 23

Only that yogi who possesses the inner Bliss, who rests on the inner Foundation, who is one with the inner Light, becomes one with Spirit (after attaining freedom from karma connected with the physical, astral, and ideational bodies). He attains complete liberation in Spirit (even while living in the body). 24

With sins obliterated, doubts removed, senses subjugated, the *rishis* (sages), contributing to the welfare of mankind, attain emancipation in Spirit. 25

Renunciants who are desireless and wrathless, mind-controlled, and Self-realized, are completely free both in this world and in the beyond. 26

A *muni* — he who holds liberation as the sole object of life and therefore frees himself from longings, fears, and wrath — controls his senses, mind, and intelligence and removes their external contacts by (a technique of) making even, or neutralizing, the currents of *prana* and *apana* that manifest as inhalation and exhalation in the nostrils. He fixes his gaze at the middle of the two eyebrows (thus converting the dual current of the physical vision into the single current of the omniscient astral eye). Such a *muni* wins complete emancipation.* 27–28

He finds peace who knows Me as the Enjoyer of the holy rites (*yajnas*) and of the austerities (offered by devotees), as the Infinite Lord of Creation, and as the Good Friend of all creatures. 29

Aum, Tat, Sat.

In the Upanishad of the holy Bhagavad Gita — the discourse of Lord Krishna to Arjuna, which is the scripture of yoga and the science of God-realization — this is the fifth chapter, called "Union Through Renunciation of the Fruits of Action."

---

* See sidebar, next page.

Kriya Yoga: The Gita's Supreme Technique of Emancipation

In these two stanzas [V:27–28], and in IV:29, the Gita leaves behind all abstractions and generalizations, and mentions the specific technique of salvation—*Kriya Yoga*....

By the special technique of *Kriya Yoga,* the ingoing breath of *prana* and the outgoing breath of *apana* are converted into cool and warm currents. In the beginning of the practice of *Kriya Yoga,* the devotee feels the cool *prana* current going up the spine and the warm *apana* current going down the spine....When the *Kriya Yogi* learns to dissolve the ingoing and outgoing breath into a perception of the cool and warm currents going up and down the spine, he then feels his body as sustained by these inner currents of life force and not by their by-product of breath....

He gradually finds that these two spinal currents become converted into one life force, magnetically drawing reinforcements of *prana* from all the bodily cells and nerves. This strengthened life current flows upward to the point between the eyebrows and is seen as the tricolored spherical astral eye: a luminous sun, in the center of which is a blue sphere encircling a bright scintillating star. Jesus referred to this "single" eye in the center of the forehead, and to the truth that the body is essentially formed of light, in the following words: "If therefore thine eye be single, thy whole body shall be full of light."...

This stanza of the Gita highlights the necessity of neutralizing or "making even" the currents of *prana* and *apana*. This effect is made possible by the practice of *Kriya Yoga,* which recharges the body cells by the inner cosmic life so that inhalation and exhalation become even—that is, still and unnecessary....Breath is still, life is still, sensations and thoughts are dissolved. The divine light of life and consciousness perceived by the devotee in the cerebrospinal centers becomes one with the Cosmic Light and Cosmic Consciousness....

By this scientific step-by-step method, the yogi ascends from the senses in actuality and not by a mere ineffectual mental diversion from them....He learns scientifically to divert to the spine and brain the currents from his five sense channels and thus to unite his consciousness with the joy of higher spiritual perceptions in the seven centers. When he is able to remain immersed in divine bliss even in his active state, he does not become further involved in desires to enjoy external objects. Radiating the calmness of divine realizations, he is not disturbed by the springing up of fear and anger from nonfulfillments of material desires. He finds his soul no longer tied to matter but forever united to the cosmic bliss of Spirit.

CHAPTER VI

Permanent Shelter in Spirit
Through Yoga Meditation

True Renunciation and True Yoga Depend on Meditation

The Blessed Lord said:

He is the true renunciant and also the true yogi who performs dutiful and spiritual actions (*karyam* and *karma*) without desiring their fruits — not he who performs no fire ceremony (sacrifice) nor he who abandons action.   1

Understand, O Pandava (Arjuna), that what is spoken of in the scriptures as renunciation is the same as yoga; for he who has not renounced selfish motive (*sankalpa*) cannot be a yogi.   2

For the *muni* desiring ascension, meditative action (*karma*) for divine union (yoga) is spoken of as "his way"; when he has mastered this yoga, then inaction is said to be "his way."   3

He who has overcome attachment both to sense objects and to actions, and who is free from all ego-instigated plannings — that man is said to have attained firm union of soul with Spirit.   4

Transforming the Little Self (Ego) Into
the Divine Self (Soul)

Let man uplift the self (ego) by the self; let the self not be self-degraded (cast down). Indeed, the self is its own friend; and the self is its own enemy.   5

For him whose self (ego) has been conquered by the Self (soul), the Self is the friend of the self; but verily, the Self behaves inimically, as an enemy, toward the self that is not subdued.*   6

The tranquil sage, victorious over the self (ego), is ever fully established in the Supreme Self (Spirit), whether he encounter cold or heat,
pleasure or pain, praise or blame.   7

That yogi who is gladly absorbed in truth and Self-realization is
said to be indissolubly united to Spirit. Unchangeable, conqueror of
his senses, he looks with an equal eye on earth, stone, and gold.   8

He is a supreme yogi who regards with equal-mindedness all
men — patrons, friends, enemies, strangers, mediators, hateful beings,
relatives, the virtuous and the ungodly.   9

Krishna's Advice for Successful Practice of Yoga

Free from ever-hoping desires and from cravings for possessions,
with the heart (waves of feeling) controlled by the soul (by yoga concentration), retiring alone to a quiet place, the yogi should constantly
try to unite with the soul.   10

The yogi's seat, in a clean place, should be firm (not wobbly), neither too high nor too low, and covered, first, with *kusha* grass, then
with a deer or tiger skin, then with a cloth.   11

Established on that seat, concentrating the mind on one point,
and controlling the activities of the fanciful faculty (*chitta*, feeling — the power that visualizes) and the senses, let him practice yoga
for self-purification.   12

Firmly holding the spine, neck, and head erect and motionless, let
the yogi focus his eyes at the starting place of the nose (the spot between
the two eyebrows); let him not gaze around in various directions.   13

With serenity and fearlessness, with steadfastness in brahmacharya, with the mind controlled, with the thoughts centered on Me,
the yogi should sit, meditating on Me as the Final Goal.   14

The self-governed yogi — he whose mind is fully under control — thus engaging his soul in ceaseless meditative union with Spirit,

* See explanation of verses 5 and 6 on pages 48–9.

attains the peace of My being: the final Nirvana (deliverance).   15

O Arjuna! The gourmand, the scanty eater, the person who habitually oversleeps, the one who sleeps too little — none of these finds success in yoga.   16

He who with proper regularity eats, relaxes, works, sleeps, and remains awake will find yoga the destroyer of suffering.   17

Attaining Self-Mastery and Control of the Mind

When the *chitta* (feeling) is absolutely subjugated and is calmly established in the Self, the yogi, thus devoid of attachment to all desires, is spoken of as the God-united.   18

The illustration of an unflickering flame of light in a windless spot may be used in reference to a yogi who has conquered his feeling (*chitta*) by the practice of meditation on the Self.   19

The state of complete tranquility of the feeling (*chitta*), attained by yoga meditation, in which the self (ego) perceives itself as the Self (soul) and is content (fixed) in the Self;   20

What Is Brahmacharya (Verse 14)?

[Commonly understood as self-control, especially of the sexual impulse, brahmacharya is one of the five *yamas* (religious proscriptions) cited as the first step of Patanjali's Eightfold Path of Yoga. Commenting on verse 14, Paramahansa Yogananda wrote:]

"He who is steadfast in *brahmacharya* is defined as a celibate student who is faithful in living a holy life, engaging in sacred study and self-discipline. In the prescribed Vedic plan, this was basically the beginning of the spiritual life for all aspirants. '*Brahmachari-vrate*' has also a deeper meaning here: literally, 'one whose sphere of action or act of devotion (*vrata*) is practicing (*chāra*) *Aum* (*brahma:* the sacred sound, *shabda-brahman*).' The accomplished brahmachari, then, is one who by the practice of meditating on *Aum* roams or progresses in the realm of Brahman manifested as the Creator or Holy Vibration: the *Aum*, Amen, or Holy Ghost.

The state in which the sense-transcendent immeasurable bliss becomes known to the awakened intuitive intelligence, and in which the yogi remains enthroned, never again to be removed;   21

The state that, once found, the yogi considers as the treasure beyond all other treasures — anchored therein, he is immune to even the mightiest grief;   22

That state is known as yoga — the pain-free state. The practice of yoga is therefore to be observed resolutely and with a stout heart.   23

Relinquish without exception all longings born of *sankalpas* (plannings), and completely control, sheerly with the mind, the sensory organs, the sensory powers, and their contact with the ubiquitous sense objects.   24

With the intuitive discrimination saturated in patience, with the mind absorbed in the soul, the yogi, freeing his mind from all thoughts, will by slow degrees attain tranquility.   25

Whenever the fickle and restless mind wanders away — for whatever reason — let the yogi withdraw it from those distractions and return it to the sole control of the Self.   26

The yogi who has completely calmed the mind and controlled the passions and freed them from all impurities,* and who is one with Spirit — verily, he has attained supreme blessedness.   27

The yogi, free from all impurities, ceaselessly engaging the Self thus in the activity of yoga (divine union), readily attains the blessedness of continuous mergence in Spirit.   28

With the soul united to Spirit by yoga, with a vision of equality for all things, the yogi beholds his Self (Spirit-united) in all creatures and all creatures in the Spirit.   29

He who perceives Me everywhere and beholds everything in Me never loses sight of Me, nor do I ever lose sight of him.   30

That yogi stays forever in Me, who, anchored in divine unity what-

---

* Literally, "*he* is freed from all impurities." The yogi himself is said to be free from all impurities when first the activities of the mind and its passions are stilled by concentration and thereby freed from the taint of dualities.

ever his mode of existence, realizes Me as pervading all beings.   31

O Arjuna, the best type of yogi is he who feels for others, whether in grief or pleasure, even as he feels for himself.   32

The Lord's Promise: The Persevering Yogi Ultimately Is Victorious

Arjuna said:

O Madhusudana (Krishna), owing to my restlessness, I do not behold the permanent enduring effect of the equalizing yoga that Thou hast related to me.   33

Verily, the mind is unsteady, tumultuous, powerful, obstinate! O Krishna, I consider the mind as difficult to master as the wind!   34

The Blessed Lord said:

O Mahabaho ("mighty-armed" Arjuna), undoubtedly the mind is fickle and unruly; but by yoga practice and by dispassion, O Son of Kunti (Arjuna), the mind may nevertheless be controlled.   35

This is My word: Yoga is difficult of attainment by the ungoverned man; but he who is self-controlled will, by striving through proper methods, be able to achieve it.   36

Arjuna said:

O Krishna! what happens to a person unsuccessful in yoga — one who has devotedly tried to meditate but has been unable to control himself because his mind kept running away during yoga practice?   37

Doesn't the yogi perish like a sundered cloud if he finds not the way to Brahman (Spirit) — being thus unsheltered in Him and steeped in delusion, sidetracked from both paths (the one of God-union and the one of right activities)?*   38

---

* Reference to the two paths cited in the first verse of this chapter, in which the yogi was described as he who follows primarily the path of ecstatic meditation for God-union; and the renunciant as he who follows the path of inner renunciation, performing dutiful and meditative actions but without attachment to or desire for their fruits. The meditative yogi who is nonattached and the active devotee of inner renunciation who meditates are both ideal yogis, pursuing a path to God-union. The present verse addresses the fate of such yogis who have not been wholly successful in their endeavors.

Please remove forever all my doubts, O Krishna! for none save Thee may banish my uncertainties.   39

The Blessed Lord said:

O Arjuna, My son! a performer of good actions never meets destruction. Whether in this world or in the beyond, he falls not into evil plight!   40

A fallen yogi, gaining entry to the world of the virtuous, remains there for many years; afterward he is reborn on earth in a good and prosperous home.   41

Or he may reincarnate in a family of enlightened yogis; verily, a birth like that is much harder to gain on this earth!   42

There, O Arjuna, he recovers the yoga discrimination attained in his former existence, and tries more strenuously for spiritual success.   43

The power of former yoga practice is sufficient to force, as it were, the yogi on his onward path. An eager student of even theoretical yoga is farther advanced than is a follower of the outward scriptural rites.   44

By diligently following his path, the yogi, perfected by the efforts of many births, is purged of sin (karmic taint) and finally enters the Supreme Beatitude.   45

The yogi is deemed greater than body-disciplining ascetics, greater even than the followers of the path of wisdom or of the path of action; be thou, O Arjuna, a yogi!*   46

He who with devotion absorbs himself in Me, with his soul immersed in Me, him I regard, among all classes of yogis, as the most equilibrated.   47

Aum, Tat, Sat.

In the Upanishad of the holy Bhagavad Gita — the discourse of Lord Krishna to Arjuna, which is the scripture of yoga and the science of God-realization — this is the sixth chapter, called "Dhyana Yoga (Union Through Meditation)."

* See explanation of this verse on pages 49 ff.

CHAPTER VII

The Nature of Spirit and the Spirit of Nature

"Hear How Thou Shalt Realize Me"

The Blessed Lord said:

O Partha (Arjuna), absorbing thy mind in Me, taking shelter in Me, and following the path of yoga — hear how thou shalt realize Me beyond all doubts, in full completion (knowing Me with all My attributes and powers).　　　　　　　　　　　　　　　1

I shall relate to thee without omission both theoretical wisdom and that wisdom which can be known only by intuitive realization — knowing which, naught in this world will remain unknown to thee.　　2

Among thousands of men, perhaps one strives for spiritual attainment; and, among the blessed true seekers that assiduously try to reach Me, perhaps one perceives Me as I am.　　　　　　　　　3

Prakriti: The Dual Nature of Spirit in Creation

My manifested nature (Prakriti) has an eightfold differentiation: earth, water, fire, air, ether, sensory mind (*manas*), intelligence (*buddhi*), and egoism (*ahamkara*).　　　　　　　　　　　4

Thus My lower nature (Apara-Prakriti). But understand, O Mighty-armed (Arjuna)! that My different and higher nature (Para-Prakriti) is the *jiva*, the self-consciousness and life-principle, that sustains the cosmos.　　　　　　　　　　　　　　　5

Understand that these dual Natures of Mine, the pure and the impure Prakriti, are the womb of all beings. I am the Progenitor and also the Dissolver of the entire cosmos.　　　　　　　　　6

How the Creator Sustains the Manifested Creation

O Arjuna! There is nothing higher than Me, or beyond Me. All things (creatures and objects) are bound to Me like a row of gems on a thread.   7

O Son of Kunti (Arjuna), I am the fluidity in waters; I am the radiation in the moon and the sun; I am the *Aum* (*pranava*) in all the Vedas; the sound in the ether; and the manliness in men.   8

I am the wholesome fragrance exuding from the earth; the luminescence in the fire am I; the life in all creatures, and the self-discipline in anchorites.   9

Know Me to be the eternal seed of all creatures, O Son of Pritha (Arjuna)! I am the understanding of the keen, the radiance of vital beings.   10

Among the powerful, O Best of the Bharatas (Arjuna), I am the power that is free from longings and attachment. I am that desire in men which is in keeping with *dharma* (righteousness).   11

Know thou that all manifestations of *sattva* (good), *rajas* (activity), and *tamas* (evil) emanate from Me. Though they are in Me, I am not in them.   12

Cosmic Hypnosis (Maya) and the Way to Transcend It

This world of mortal beings does not perceive Me, unchangeable and beyond all qualities, because they are deluded by the triple modes of Nature.   13

It is difficult indeed to go beyond the influence of My divine cosmic hypnosis, imbued with the triple qualities. Only those who take shelter in Me (the Cosmic Hypnotizer) become free from this power of illusion.   14

The lowest of men, perpetrators of evil and misguided fools, whose discrimination has been stolen by *maya* (delusion), follow the path of demoniac beings, failing to take shelter in Me.   15

The afflicted, the questers for wisdom, the cravers for power here and in the hereafter,* and the wise — these, O Arjuna, are the four kinds of righteous men who pursue Me. 16

Chief among them is the sage, ever constant and one-pointed in devotion. For I am exceedingly dear to the sage, and he is exceedingly dear to Me. 17

All these (four kinds of men) are noble, but the sage I consider indeed as My own Self. Unwaveringly is he settled in Me alone as his utmost goal. 18

After many incarnations, the sage attains Me, realizing, "The Lord is all-pervading!" A man so illumined is hard to find. 19

Which "God" Should Be Worshiped?

Led by their own inclinations, their discrimination stolen by this or that craving, pursuing this or that cultic injunction, men seek lesser gods. 20

Whatever embodiment (a God-incarnate, a saint, or a deity) a devotee strives faithfully to worship, it is I who make his devotion unflinching. 21

Absorbed in that devotion, intent on the worship of that embodiment, the devotee thus gains the fruits of his longings. Yet those fulfillments are verily granted by Me alone. 22

But men of scant knowledge (worshiping lesser gods) receive limited results. The devotees of the deities go unto them; My devotees come unto Me. 23

Men without wisdom consider Me, the Unmanifest, as assuming embodiment (like a mortal being taking a form) — not understanding My unsurpassable state, My unchangeable unutterable nature. 24

Perceiving the Spirit Behind the Dream-Shadows of Nature

Seemingly eclipsed by My own *Yoga-Maya* (the delusion born of

---

* *Artharthi,* lit., "he who has a strong desire to attain his aim or object"; that is, he who craves the power of fulfillment in the present and in the hereafter.

the triple qualities in Nature), I am unseen by men. The bewildered world knows not Me, the Unborn, the Deathless.   25

O Arjuna, I am aware of the creatures of the past, the present, and the future; but Me no one knows.   26

O Descendant of Bharata, Scorcher of Foes (Arjuna)! at birth all creatures are immersed in delusive ignorance (*moha*) by the delusion of the pairs of opposites springing from longing and aversion.   27

But righteous men, their sins obliterated, and subject no longer to the oppositional delusions, worship Me steadfastly.   28

Those who seek deliverance from decay and death by clinging to Me know Brahman (the Absolute), the all-inclusiveness of *Adhyatma* (the soul as the repository of Spirit), and all secrets of karma.   29

Those who perceive Me in the *Adhibhuta* (the physical), the *Adhidaiva* (the astral), and the *Adhiyajna* (the spiritual), with heart united to the soul, continue to perceive Me even at the time of death.   30

Aum, Tat, Sat.

In the Upanishad of the holy Bhagavad Gita — the discourse of Lord Krishna to Arjuna, which is the scripture of yoga and the science of God-realization — this is the seventh chapter, called "The Yoga of Knowledge and Discriminative Wisdom."

CHAPTER VIII

The Imperishable Absolute: Beyond the Cycles of Creation and Dissolution

The Manifestations of Spirit in the Macrocosm and Microcosm

Arjuna said:

O Best of the Purushas (Krishna)! Please tell me, what is Brahman (Spirit)? What is *Adhyatma* (the *Kutastha* Consciousness underlying all manifestations and existing as the souls of all beings in the cosmos)? And what is Karma (cosmic and meditative actions born of *Aum*)? What is *Adhibhuta* (the consciousness immanent in physical creatures and the physical cosmos)? And what is *Adhidaiva* (the consciousness manifest in astral bodies and the astral cosmos)?   1

O Slayer of the Demon Madhu (Krishna)! What is *Adhiyajna* (the Supreme Creative and Cognizing Spirit), and in what manner is *Adhiyajna* present (as the soul) in this body? And how, at the time of death, art Thou to be known by the self-disciplined?   2

The Blessed Lord replied:

The Indestructible and Supreme Spirit is Brahman. Its undifferentiated manifestation (as *Kutastha Chaitanya* and as the individual soul) is called *Adhyatma*. The *Aum* (Cosmic Vibration or the *Visarga*) that causes the birth and sustenance and dissolution of beings and their various natures is termed Karma (cosmic action).   3

O Supreme Among the Embodied (Arjuna)! *Adhibhuta* is the basis of physical existence; *Adhidaiva* is the basis of astral existence; and I the Spirit within the body and the cosmos am *Adhiyajna* (the Causal Origin, the Great Sacrificer, the Maker and Cognizer of all).   4

The Yogi's Experience at the Time of Death

Lastly, he enters My Being who thinks only of Me at the hour of his passing, when the body is abandoned. This is truth beyond doubt.   5

O Son of Kunti (Arjuna), that thought with which a dying man leaves the body determines — through his long persistence in it — his next state of being.   6

Therefore, remember Me always, and engage thyself in the battle of activity! Surrender to Me thy mind and thine understanding! Thus without doubt shalt thou come unto Me.   7

He attains the Supreme Effulgent Lord, O Partha (Arjuna), whose mind, stabilized by yoga, is immovably fixed on the thought of Him.   8

At the time of death a yogi reaches the Supreme Effulgent Lord if, with love and by the power of yoga, he fully penetrates his life force between the eyebrows (the seat of the spiritual eye), and if he fixes his mind unwaveringly on the Being who, beyond all delusions of darkness, shines like the sun — the One whose form is unimaginable, subtler than the finest atom, the Supporter of all, the Great Ruler, eternal and omniscient.   9–10

The Method of Attaining the Supreme

That which the Vedic seers declare as the Immutable, That which is gained by renunciants of vanished attachments, desiring which they lead a life of self-discipline — the method for attaining That I will relate to thee in brief.   11

He who closes the nine gates of the body,* who cloisters the mind in the heart center, who fixes the full life force in the cerebrum — he who thus engages in the steady practice of yoga, establishing himself in *Aum*, the Holy Word of Brahman, and remembering Me (Spirit) at the time of his final exit from the body, reaches the Highest Goal.   12–13

---

* *Sarvadvārāṇi deham*, "all gates of the body." These were identified in verse V:13 as nine in number: "the bodily city of nine gates." They consist of the two eyes, two ears, two nostrils, the two organs of excretion and of procreation, and the mouth.

O Partha (Arjuna)! I am easily reached by that yogi who is single-hearted, who remembers Me daily, continually, his mind intensely focused only on Me.   14

My noble devotees, having obtained Me (Spirit), have reached supreme success; they incur no further rebirths in this abode of grief and transitoriness.   15

The Cycles of Cosmic Creation

Yogis not yet free from the world revolve back again (to the world) even from the high sphere of Brahma (union with God in *samadhi*). But on entering into Me (the transcendental Spirit) there is no rebirth, O son of Kunti (Arjuna)!*   16

They are true knowers of "day" and "night" who understand the Day of Brahma, which endures for a thousand cycles (*yugas*), and the Night of Brahma, which also endures for a thousand cycles.   17

At the dawn of Brahma's Day all creation, reborn, emerges from the state of nonmanifestation; at the dusk of Brahma's Night all creation sinks into the sleep of nonmanifestation.   18

Again and again, O son of Pritha (Arjuna), the same throng of men helplessly take rebirth. Their series of incarnations ceases at the coming of Night, and then reappears at the dawn of Day.   19

But transcending the unmanifested (states of phenomenal being) there exists the true Unmanifested, the Immutable, the Absolute, which remains untouched by the cycles of cosmic dissolution.   20

The aforesaid Unmanifested, the Immutable Absolute, is thus called the Supreme Goal. Those who attain it, My highest state, undergo no more rebirth.   21

By singlehearted devotion, O son of Pritha (Arjuna), that Supreme

---

* The Sanskrit word *lokas* translated in this verse as "human beings" (i.e., those who yet possess mortal consciousness) may also be rendered as "worlds." With that interpretation, the verse translates as follows, and leads into the succeeding verses:

   "All worlds, from the high sphere of Brahma (to the gross earth), are subject to (the finite law of) recurrence. But those devotees, O Arjuna! who become merged in Me are freed from rebirth."

Unmanifested is reached. He alone, the Omnipresent, is the Abode of all creatures.   22

The Way of Release From the Cycles of Rebirth

I shall now declare unto thee, O Best of the Bharatas (Arjuna), the path, traversing which at the time of death, yogis attain freedom; and also the path wherein there is rebirth.*   23

Fire, light, daytime, the bright half of the lunar month, the six months of the northern course of the sun — pursuing this path at the time of departure, the knowers of God go to God.   24

Smoke, nighttime, the dark half of the lunar month, the six months of the southern course of the sun — he who follows this path obtains only the lunar light and then returns to earth.   25

These two paths for exiting from the world are reckoned eternal. The way of light leads to release, the way of darkness leads to rebirth.   26

No yogi who understands these two paths is ever deluded (into following the way of darkness). Therefore, O Arjuna! at all times maintain thyself firmly in yoga.   27

He who knows the truth about the two paths gains merit far beyond any implicit in the study of the scriptures, or in sacrifices, or in penances, or in gift-giving. That yogi reaches his Supreme Origin.   28

Aum, Tat, Sat.

In the Upanishad of the holy Bhagavad Gita — the discourse of Lord Krishna to Arjuna, which is the scripture of yoga and the science of God-realization — this is the eighth chapter, called "Union With the Absolute Spirit."

---

* As explained in the lengthy commentary in *God Talks With Arjuna,* verses 23–28 are deeply symbolic references to the science of yoga and cannot be understood by a literal reading.

CHAPTER IX

The Royal Knowledge, The Royal Mystery

Direct Perception of God, Through Methods
of Yoga "Easy to Perform"

The Blessed Lord said:

To thee, the uncarping one, I shall now reveal the sublime mystery (the immanent-transcendent nature of Spirit). Possessing intuitive realization of this wisdom, thou shalt escape from evil.   1

This intuitive realization is the king of sciences, the royal secret, the peerless purifier, the essence of *dharma* (man's righteous duty); it is the direct perception of truth — the imperishable enlightenment — attained through ways (of yoga) very easy to perform.   2

Men without faith in this *dharma* (without devotion to the practices that bestow realization) attain Me not, O Scorcher of Foes (Arjuna)! Again and again they tread the death-darkened path of *samsara* (the rounds of rebirth).   3

How the Lord Pervades All Creation,
Yet Remains Transcendent

I, the Unmanifested, pervade the whole universe. All creatures abide in Me, but I do not abide in them.   4

Behold My Divine Mystery! in which all beings are apparently not in Me, nor does My Self dwell in them; yet I alone am their Creator and Preserver!   5

Understand it thus: Just as air moves freely in the infinitudes of space (*akasha*), and has its being in space (yet air is different from space), just so do all creatures have their being in Me (but they are not I).   6

At the end of a cycle (*kalpa*), O Son of Kunti (Arjuna), all beings return to the unmanifested state of My Cosmic Nature (Prakriti). At the beginning of the next cycle, again I cast them forth.   7

By revivifying Prakriti, Mine own emanation, again and again I produce this host of creatures, all subject to the finite laws of Nature.   8

But these activities entrammel Me not, O Winner of Wealth (Arjuna), for I remain above them, aloof and unattached.   9

O Son of Kunti (Arjuna), it is solely My impregnating presence that causes Mother Nature to give birth to the animate and the inanimate. Because of Me (through Prakriti) the worlds revolve in alternating cycles (of creation and dissolution).   10

The ignorant, oblivious of My transcendental nature as the Maker of all creatures, discount also My presence within the human form.   11

Lacking in insight, their desires and thoughts and actions all vain, such men possess the deluded nature of fiends and demons.   12

But *mahatmas* ("great souls"), O Son of Pritha (Arjuna), expressing in their nature divine qualities, offer the homage of their undeviating minds to Me, knowing Me as the imperishable Source of all life.   13

Constantly absorbed in Me, bowing low with adoration, fixed and resolute in their high aspiration, they worship Me and ever praise My name.   14

Others, also, performing the *yajna* of knowledge, worship Me, the Cosmic-Bodied Lord, in various ways — first as the Many, and then as the One.   15

I am the rite, the sacrifice, the oblation to ancestors, the medicinal herb, the holy chant, the melted butter, the sacred fire, and the offering.   16

Of this world I am the Father, the Mother, the Ancestor, the Preserver, the Sanctifier, the all-inclusive Object of Knowledge, the Cosmic *Aum,* and also the Vedic lore.   17

I am the Ultimate Goal, the Upholder, the Master, the Witness, the Shelter, the Refuge, and the One Friend. I am the Origin, the Dissolution, the Foundation, the Cosmic Storehouse, and the Seed Indestructible. 18

I bestow solar heat, O Arjuna, and give or withhold the rain. Immortality am I, and also Death; I am Being (*Sat*) and Non-Being (*Asat*). 19

The Right Method of Worshiping God

The Veda-ritualists, cleansing themselves of sin by the *soma* rite, worship Me by *yajna* (sacrifice), and thus win their desire of entry into heaven. There, in the sacred kingdom of the astral deities, devotees enjoy the subtle celestial pleasures. 20

But after delighting in the glorious higher regions, such beings, at the expiration of their good karma, return to earth. Thus abiding by the scriptural regulations, desiring the enjoyments (the promised celestial rewards thereof), they travel the cyclic path (between heaven and earth). 21

To men who meditate on Me as their Very Own, ever united to Me by incessant worship, I supply their deficiencies and make permanent their gains. 22

O Son of Kunti (Arjuna), even devotees of other gods, who sacrifice to them with faith, worship Me alone, though not in the right way. 23

I am indeed the only Enjoyer and Lord of all sacrifices. But they (the worshipers of My lesser forms) do not perceive Me in My true nature; hence, they fall. 24

Devotees of the astral deities go to them; ancestor worshipers go to the manes; to the nature spirits go those who seek them; but My devotees come to Me. 25

The reverent presentation to Me of a leaf, a flower, a fruit, or water, given with pure intention, is a devotional offering acceptable in My sight. 26

Whatever actions thou dost perform, O Son of Kunti (Arjuna), whether in eating, or in observing spiritual rites, or in gift bestowing, or in self-disciplining — dedicate them all as offerings to Me.   27

Thus no action of thine can enchain thee with good or evil karma. With thy Self steadfastly anchored in Me by Yoga and renunciation, thou shalt win freedom and come unto Me.   28

I am impartial toward all beings. To Me none is hateful, none is dear. But those who give Me their heart's love are in Me, as I am in them.   29

Even a consummate evildoer who turns away from all else to worship Me exclusively may be counted among the good, because of his righteous resolve.   30

He will fast become a virtuous man and obtain unending peace. Tell all assuredly, O Arjuna, that My devotee never perishes!   31

Taking shelter in Me all beings can achieve the Supreme Fulfillment — be they those of sinful birth, or women, or Vaishyas, or Sudras.   32

How easily, then, may I be attained by sainted Brahmins (knowers of God or Brahman) and pious royal sages (*Rajarishis*)! Thou who hast entered this impermanent and unhappy world, adore only Me (Spirit).   33

On Me fix thy mind, be thou My devotee, with ceaseless worship bow reverently before Me. Having thus united thyself to Me as thy Highest Goal, thou shalt be Mine own.   34

Aum, Tat, Sat.

In the Upanishad of the holy Bhagavad Gita — the discourse of Lord Krishna to Arjuna, which is the scripture of yoga and the science of God-realization — this is the ninth chapter, called "Union Through the Royal Knowledge and the Royal Mystery."

CHAPTER X

The Infinite Manifestations of the Unmanifest Spirit

The Unborn and Beginningless, Beyond Form and Conception

The Blessed Lord said:

O Mighty-Armed (Arjuna), hear thou more of My supreme utterance. For thy highest good I will speak further to thee, who listeneth joyfully.   1

Neither the multitude of angels nor the great sages know My Uncreated Nature, for even the *devas* and *rishis* (are created beings, and hence) have an origin in Me.   2

But whoever realizes Me to be the Unborn and Beginningless as well as the Sovereign Lord of Creation — that man has conquered delusion and attained the sinless state even while wearing a mortal body.   3

The Diverse Modifications of God's Nature

Discrimination, wisdom, lack of delusion, forgiveness, truth, control of the senses, peace of mind, joy, sorrow, birth, death, fear, courage, harmlessness, equanimity, serenity, self-discipline, charity, fame, and infamy — these diverse states of beings spring from Me alone as modifications of My nature.   4–5

The seven Great Rishis, the Primeval Four, and the (fourteen) Manus are also modifications of My nature, born of My thought, and endowed with (creative) powers like Mine. From these progenitors come all living creatures on earth.   6

He who realizes by yoga the truth of My prolific manifestations and the creative and dissolving power of My Divine Yoga is unshakably united to Me. This is beyond doubt.   7

I am the Source of everything; from Me all creation emerges. With this realization the wise, awestricken, adore Me.   8

Their thoughts fully on Me, their beings surrendered to Me, enlightening one another, proclaiming Me always, My devotees are contented and joyful.   9

To those thus ever attached to Me, and who worship Me with love, I impart that discriminative wisdom (*buddhi yoga*) by which they attain Me utterly.   10

From sheer compassion I, the Divine Indweller, set alight in them the radiant lamp of wisdom which banishes the darkness that is born of ignorance.   11

The Devotee Prays to Hear From the Lips of the Lord Himself: "What Are Thy Many Aspects and Forms?"

Arjuna said:

The Supreme Spirit, the Supreme Shelter, the Supreme Purity art Thou! All the great sages, the divine seer Narada, as well as Asita, Devala, and Vyasa, have thus described Thee as the Self-Evolved Eternal Being, the Original Deity, uncaused and omnipresent. And now Thou Thyself tellest me!   12–13

O Keshava (Krishna)! I consider as eternal truth all Thou hast revealed to me. Indeed, O my Lord! neither the Devas (gods) nor the Danavas (Titans) know the infinite modes of Thine appearances.   14

O Divine Purusha, O Origin of beings, O Lord of all creatures, O God of gods, O Sustainer of the world! verily Thou alone knowest Thyself by Thyself.   15

Therefore, please tell me exhaustively of Thy divine powers and qualities by which Thine Omnipresence sustaineth the cosmos.   16

O Great Yogi (Krishna)! how shall I always meditate in order to know Thee truly? In what aspects and forms, O Blessed Lord, art Thou to be conceived by me?   17

O Janardana (Krishna)! tell me more, at great length, of Thy yoga powers and Self-manifestations; for never can I hear enough of Thy nectared speech!   18

"I Will Tell Thee of My Phenomenal Expressions"

The Blessed Lord said:

Very well, O Best of the Princes (Arjuna), I will indeed tell thee of My phenomenal expressions — but only the most outstanding ones, for there is no end to My variety.   19

O Conqueror of Sleep (Arjuna)! I am the Self in the heart of all creatures: I am their Origin, Existence, and Finality.   20

Among the Adityas (twelve effulgent beings), I am Vishnu; among luminaries, I am the radiating sun; among the Maruts (forty-nine wind gods), I am Marichi; among heavenly bodies, I am the moon.   21

Among the Vedas, I am the Sama Veda; among the gods, I am Vasava (Indra); among the senses, I am mind (*manas*); in creatures, I am the intelligence.   22

Of the Rudras (eleven radiant beings) I am (their leader) Shankara ("the well-wisher"); of the Yakshas and Rakshasas (astral demi-goblins), I am Kubera (lord of riches); of the Vasus (eight vitalizing beings), I am Pavaka (the god of fire, the purifying power); and of mountain peaks I am Meru.   23

And, O son of Pritha (Arjuna), understand Me to be the chief among priests, Brihaspati; among generals, I am Skanda; among expanses of water, I am the ocean.   24

Of the Maharishis (mighty sages), I am Bhrigu; among words, I am the one syllable *Aum;* among *yajnas* (holy ceremonies), I am *japa-yajna* (silent, superconscious chanting); among stationary objects, I am the Himalaya.   25

Among all trees, I am the Ashvattha (the holy fig tree); among the *devarishis* (divine sages), I am Narada; among the Gandharvas (demi-gods), I am Chitraratha; among the *siddhas* (successful liberated beings), I am the *muni* (saint) Kapila.   26

Among stallions, know Me to be the nectar-born Uchchaihshravas; among elephants, Indra's white elephant, Airavata; and among men, the emperor.   27

Among weapons, I am the thunderbolt; of bovines, I am Kamadhuk (the celestial cow that fulfills all desires). I am Kandarpa (the personified creative consciousness), the cause of childbirths; and I am Vasuki among serpents.   28

I am Ananta ("the eternal" one) among the Naga serpents; I am Varuna (god of the ocean) among water creatures; I am Aryama among Pitris (ancestral parents); I am Yama (god of death) among all controllers.   29

Among the Daityas (demons and giants), I am Prahlada; among measurers, I am time; among the animals, I am the king of beasts (the lion); and among birds, I am Garuda ("lord of the skies," vehicle of Vishnu).   30

Among purifiers, I am the breeze; among wielders of weapons, I am Rama; among aquatic creatures, I am Makara (vehicle of the god of the ocean); among streams, I am Jahnavi (the Ganges).   31

Of all manifestations, O Arjuna, I am the beginning, middle, and end. Among all branches of knowledge, I am the wisdom of the Self; for debaters, I am discriminative logic (*vada*).   32

Among all letters, I am the letter A; of all compounds, I am the *dvandva* (connective element). I am Immutable Time; and I am the Omnipresent Creator (the all-pervading Dispenser of Destiny) whose face is turned on all sides.   33

I am all-dissolving Death; and I am Birth, the origin of all that will be. Among feminine manifestations (qualities of Prakriti), I am fame, success, the illumining power of speech, memory, discriminative intelligence, the grasping faculty of intuition, and the steadfastness of divine forbearance.   34

Among Samas (hymns), I am Brihat-Saman; among poetic meters, I am Gayatri; among the months, I am Margasirsha (an auspicious winter month); among seasons, I am Kusumakara, the flower-bearer (Spring).   35

I am the gambling of the practicers of fraud; I am the radiance of the radiant; I am victory and the striving power; I am the quality of *sattva* among the good.   36

Among the Vrishnis, I am Vasudeva (Krishna); among the Pandavas, I am Dhananjaya (Arjuna); among the *munis* (saints), I am Vyasa; among the sages, I am the savant Ushanas.   37

I am the rod of the discipliners; I am the art of those who seek victory; I am also the silence of all hidden things, and the wisdom of all knowers.   38

I am, furthermore, whatsoever constitutes the reproductive seed of all beings. There is nothing, O Arjuna, moving or motionless, that can abide without Me.   39

O Scorcher of Foes (Arjuna), limitless are the manifestations of My divine attributes; My concise declaration is a mere intimation of My proliferating glorious powers.   40

Any being that is a worker of miracles, that is a possessor of true prosperity, that is endowed with great prowess, know all such to be manifested sparks of My radiance.   41

But what need hast thou, O Arjuna, for the manifold details of this wisdom? (Understand simply:) I, the Unchanging and Everlasting, sustain and permeate the entire cosmos with but one fragment of My Being!   42

Aum, Tat, Sat.

In the Upanishad of the holy Bhagavad Gita — the discourse of Lord Krishna to Arjuna, which is the scripture of yoga and the science of God-realization — this is the tenth chapter, called "Vibhuti Yoga (Divine Manifestations)."

CHAPTER XI

Vision of Visions: The Lord Reveals His Cosmic Form

Arjuna said:

Thou hast compassionately revealed to me the secret wisdom of the true Self, thus banishing my delusion.   1

O Lotus-Eyed (Krishna)! Thou hast told me extensively of the beginning and end of all beings, and of Thine eternal sovereignty.   2

O Great One! truly hast Thou thus declared Thyself. Yet, O Purushottama! I long to see Thee in Divine Embodiment (Thine Ishvara-Form).   3

O Master, O Lord of Yogis! if Thou deemest me able to see It, show to me Thine Infinite Self!   4

God as Ishvara: Ruler of the Cosmos

Hindu scriptures contain a thousand names for God, each one conveying a different shade of philosophical meaning. Purushottama (XI:3) or "Supreme Spirit" is an appellation for Deity in His highest aspect — the Unmanifested Lord beyond creation. Ishvara (XI:3) is God in His aspect of Cosmic Ruler (from the verb root *īś,* to rule). Ishvara is He by whose will all universes, in orderly cycles, are created, maintained, and dissolved.

Although Arjuna fully accepts the truth of the Lord as Purushottama, his human heart yearns to see Him as Ishvara, the Divine Ruler whose body is the universe....

The Lord has no form, but in His aspect as Ishvara He assumes every form. By virtue of His supreme Yoga Power, the Unmanifested becomes the visible miracle of the universe.

The Blessed Lord said:

Behold, O son of Pritha (Arjuna)! by hundreds and by thousands My divine forms — multicolored, omnifarious!   5

Behold the Adityas, the Vasus, the Rudras, the twin Ashvins, the Maruts, and many wonders hitherto unknown!   6

Here and now, O Conqueror of Sleep (Arjuna)! behold as unified in My Cosmic Body all worlds, all that moves or is motionless, and whatever else thou desirest to see.   7

But thou canst not see Me with mortal eyes. Therefore I give thee sight divine. Behold My supreme power of yoga!   8

Sanjaya said (to King Dhritarashtra):

With these words Hari (Krishna), the exalted Lord of Yoga, revealed to Arjuna the Consummate Embodiment, the Cosmic-Bodied Ishvara-Form.   9

Arjuna saw the multifarious marvelous Presence of the Deity — infinite in forms, shining in every direction of space, omnipotence all-pervading, adorned with countless celestial robes and garlands and ornaments, upraising heavenly weapons, fragrant with every lovely essence, His mouths and eyes everywhere!   10–11

If a thousand suns appeared simultaneously in the sky, their light might dimly resemble the splendor of that Omnific Being!   12

There, resting within the infinite Form of the God of gods, Arjuna beheld the entire universe with all its diversified manifestations.   13

Then the Winner of Wealth (Arjuna), wonder-struck, his hair standing on end, his palms together in a prayerful gesture, bowing his head in awe before the Lord, addressed Him: 14

Arjuna said: 15–34

Beloved Lord,
Adored of gods!
Behold,
Thy body holds
All fleshly tenants, seers fine,

And diverse angel-gods divine.
Dwelling deep in mystery cave,
The Serpent Nature's forceful crave,*
Though fierce and subtle, now is tame,
Forgetful of her deadly game;
And Sovran Brahma, God of gods,
On lotus seat is snug secured.

Great Cosmic-Bodied Lord of worlds,
Oh, I behold, again behold
Thee all and everywhere,
Thy countless arms, trunks, mouths, and eyes!
Yet drooping, dark, my knowledge lies
About Thy birth and reign and ending here.

This day,
O Blazing, Furious Flame,
O Blinding Ray,
Thy focused power's aglow: Thy Name†
Spreads everywhere
To dark'st abysmal lair.
Gilded with a crown of stars
And wielding mace of sovereign power,
Thou whirlest forth, O Burning Phoebus,
Thine evolution's circling discus.

Immortal Brahma, all Supreme,
Thou Cosmic Shelter, Wisdom's Theme,
Eternal Dharma's Guardian true,
Thou diest not I ever knew!

O Birthless, Fleshless, Deathless One,
I see Thine endless, working arms,

* *Uragan divyan:* "celestial serpents"; reference to the creative forces that have their origin in the *kundalini*, the coiled life energy in the base center of the spine that enlivens the sense faculties when it flows down and outward into the body, but which bestows enlightenment when "tamed" and uplifted to the higher centers of spiritual perception.

†The cosmic vibratory light of *Aum*, the holy "Name" of God.

Thine ever-watching eyes
Of suns and moons, the staring skies;
And from Thy mouth spumes throbbing flame,*
As utterest Thou the *Aum,* Thy Cosmic Name.
Thy Self-born luster shields from harm,
And all creation, distance-flung, doth warm.

O Sovereign Soul! 'twixt earth and home of gods,
Directions all, and earthly sods,
All high abodes and all encircling spheres,
By Thee pervaded, far and near.
The worlds-triune awestruck by fear,
Thy dreadful wondrous form adore.

In Thee the gods their entry make;
With folded hands, afraid, some pray to shelter take
In Thee. The seers great, and heaven's-path successful ones,
With superb chants of "Peace!" do worship Thee and Thee alone.

Th'eleven lamps of heaven;
The twelve bright suns;
The grizzly eight,
The starry lusters great;
Aspiring hermits; patron gods,
The agents of the cosmic lords;
The twin-born princes strong,
Of valor known so long;
Two-score and nine noil breezes' force,
That binds the atom close;
The long-passed guardian spirits all;
The demigoblins, demigods, and demons tall;
And mighty ones in Spirit's path,†

* *Hutasha,* "fire" and *vaktra,* "mouth or organs of speech" from *vach,* "voice, utterance."

† *"Eleven lamps":* the Rudras. *"Twelve suns":* the Adityas. *"Grizzly eight":* the Vasus. *"Aspiring hermits":* Vishvedevas (godly beings honored for their austerities in the Himalayas). *"Patron gods":* Sadhyas (a class of lesser deities). *"Twin-born princes":* the Ashvins ("physicians of heaven," the gods of morning twilight heralding the dawn—thus representing the mixture of light and darkness or duality; as such, they were mythically the fathers of the Pandu princes Sahadeva

In wonder gaze upon Thy blazoned worth.

I Thee behold, Colossal-Armed!
With starry eyes and countless cheeks,
With endless hands, and legs adorned with lotus feet.
Thy chasmed mouth with doomsday's teeth
Doth yawn to swallow swooning worlds above, beneath,
And leaves a distilled joyous awe in me:
Thy grandeur I and all are wonder-struck to see!

To view the bowels of the void deep all filled with Thee —
Thy gaping mouth and diverse hues of fiery lustrous body —
O Vishnu of the flaming sight,
Thou quite o'erpowerest me, my peace dost fright.

Ferocious teeth and deadly fires do howl
In mouths of Thine that at me scowl.
Directions four are lost and gone;
Compassion show! I find no peace alone;
O Cosmic Guardian, Lord of gods,
Be pleased t'accept my humble pleading words.

The sons of senses swayed with kingly pride,
With ego, karmic habit, worldly lure, abide
And wait to leap upon our wisdom's chiefs;*
And yet they all do ride
The race of death, to fall and hide
Fore'er in Thy devouring mouth,
Adorned with crushing cruel teeth uncouth.
The victor and the vanquished must
(Thine offspring both, the righteous and ungodly ones)
Thy love still claim; yet all some day shall kiss the dust,

---

and Nakula). *"Two-score and nine breezes"*: the Maruts. *"Long-passed guardian spirits"*: the Manes (Ushmapas). *"Demigoblins, demigods, demons tall"*: Yakshas, Gandharvas, Asuras, respectively. *"Mighty ones in Spirit's path"*: Siddhas ("perfected ones").

* *"Sons of senses"*: Offspring of the Kuru King Dhritarashtra (symbolically, the blind sense-mind with its one-hundred sense proclivities led by material desire); *"Ego"*: Bhishma; *"Karmic habit"*: Drona; *"Worldly lure"*: Karna (material attraction and attachment). *"Wisdom's chiefs"*: the Pandavas (symbolically, the divine discriminative forces).

And sleep on common floor of earth.
The shattered skulls of some are seen,
As caught Thy greedy teeth between.

As diverse, restless, watery waves
Of river branches all do crave
To force through crowded wavelets' way
And meet where Neptune's home long lay,
E'en so, heroic streams of life
Do plunge to meet in maddest strife
Within Thy foaming mouth of flaming sea,
Where sparks of lives all dance in Thee.

As insects lost in beauty's game
All swiftly, thoughtless, rush to flame,
So fog-born passion's fires pretend
To glow like heavenly light of Thine,
And draw on mortals to attend
The trumpet call to deathly line.

Thy mouth ablaze
Doth bring to gaze
Its leaping tongues to lick
The angry blood of strong and weak;
Thou, Gourmand God, dost eat
With hunger infinite.
O Vishnu, Thou dost scorch
The worlds with all-pervading fiery torch.

Be pleased, O First of gods;
I ache to know, Primeval Lord,
True who Thou art — O Fiery Mood,
Yet so benign and good.
Oh, tell to me Thy Royal Will;
For it I know not still.

The Blessed Lord then said:
In guise of Endless Doom

I come as avaricious Time to seize and room
In burning maw
Of Mine the weaklings' awe,
And all the mortal meat
Of weary worlds of deathly change, and treat
Them with My nectar-life
To new and fearless, better strife.
E'en if thou dost forbear to slay
Thy wicked foes, still they — and warriors all in brave array —
Will sure and certain timely have to fall,
Ah, in My righteous teeth-of-law, withal.

Arise, awake! Arise, awake!
Dash thou upon the foe, the flesh a captive make;*
And win the victor's fame
With battle-hunted game;
Wealth of the King
Of Peace, and heaven's kingdom, bring!
I know right now the happenings all
That mystic future forth doth call;
And thus thy foes and warriors true,
Long, long ago I slew,
Ere shalt thine agent-hand
(That I would wield to land
Thy foes on death's dim shore). Now understand!

My agent thou;
Oh, this is how
I work My plans — the universe —
Through instruments diverse;
'Tis I who slew and yet will slay the senses' train†
Through thee, as through both past and future ones,
My soldiers sane!   15 – 34

---

* Reference to the battle of Kurukshetra as an allegory of the war between the forces of good and evil, not only in the macrocosm, but within the body and consciousness of man.

† *"The senses' train"*: Reference to "Drona, Bhishma, Jayadratha (attachment to mortal existence), Karna, and others." See explanation of allegory, pages 28–31.

Sanjaya said (to King Dhritarashtra):

After hearing the words of Keshava (the *maya*-transcendent Krishna), the diademed one (Arjuna, haloed with cosmic vision), trembling and awestricken, joining his palms in worshipful supplication, again made humble obeisance and addressed Krishna in a quavering voice.   35

Arjuna said:

O Hrishikesha (Krishna)! Rightly are the worlds proud and gladdened to exude Thy glory! The demons, terrified, seek safety in distance; while the multitudes of *siddhas* (perfected beings) bow down to worship Thee.   36

And why should they not pay Thee homage, O Vast Spirit? For greater art Thou than Brahma the Creator, who issued from Thee. O Infinite One, O God of gods, O Shelter of the Universe, Thou art the Imperishable — the Manifested, the Unmanifested, and That beyond (the Ultimate Mystery).   37

The Primal God art Thou! the Pristine Spirit, the Final Refuge of the Worlds, the Knower and the Known, the Supreme Fulfillment! Thine Omnipresence shines in the universe, O Thou of Inexhaustible Form!   38

O Flowing Life of Cosmic Currents (Vayu), O King of Death (Yama), O God of Flames (Agni), O Sovereign of Sea and Sky (Varuna),

Vision of Visions—A Poetic Translation

Through the portals of this song of praise, oft have I entered the Cosmic Temple to worship at the altar of the Manifested Lord. Many years ago, after one such experience in cosmic consciousness, I wrote the "Vision of Visions," a lyrical rendition of these verses [15–34] interwoven with an interpretation of their significance. I have offered this rendering herewith, rather than a more constrained verse-by-verse literal translation, in the conviction that the unique animation of feelings characteristic of poesy is a proper medium for the eloquence of this Sanskrit scriptural canticle.

O Lord of Night (the Moon), O Divine Father of Countless Offspring (Prajapati), O Ancestor of All! To Thee praise, praise without end! To Thee my salutations thousandfold!   39

O Endless Might, O Invincible Omniscient Omnipresence, O All-in-All! I bow to Thee in front and behind, I bow to Thee on the left and the right, I bow to Thee above and beneath, I bow to Thee enclosing me everywhere!   40

Unaware of this, Thy Cosmic Glory, and thinking of Thee as a familiar companion, often have I audaciously hailed Thee as "Friend" and "Krishna" and "Yadava." For all such words, whether spoken carelessly or with affection;   41

And for any irreverence I have displayed toward Thee, O Unshakable Lord! in lighthearted mood at mealtimes or while walking or sitting or resting, alone with Thee or in others' company — for all such unintentional slights, O Thou Illimitable! I beg forgiveness.   42

Father of All art Thou! of animate and inanimate alike. None but Thee is worthy of worship, O Guru Sublime! Unparalleled by any other in the three worlds, who may surpass Thee, O Lord of Power Incomparable?   43

Therefore, O Adorable One, I cast myself in obeisance at Thy feet to implore Thy pardon. As a father to his son, as a friend to a close friend, as a lover to his beloved, do Thou, O Lord, forgive me!   44

Overjoyed am I at having gazed upon a vision never seen before, yet my mind is not free from terror. Be merciful to me, O Lord of gods, O Shelter of the Worlds! Show to me only Thy Deva-form (as the benign Vishnu).   45

I long to see Thee as before, as the Four-Armed Vishnu, diademed and holding Thy mace and discus. Reappear in that same form, O Thou who art Thousand-Armed and Universe-Bodied!   46

The Blessed Lord said:

I have graciously exercised Mine own Yoga Power to reveal to thee, O Arjuna, and to none other! this Supreme Primeval Form of Mine, the Radiant and Infinite Cosmos!   47

No mortal man, save only thyself, O Great Hero of the Kurus! is able to look upon My Universal Shape—not by sacrifices or charity or works or rigorous austerity or study of the Vedas is that vision attainable.   48

Be not affrighted or stupefied at seeing My Terrible Aspect. With dreads removed and heart rejoicing, behold once more My familiar form!   49

Sanjaya said (to King Dhritarashtra):

After speaking thus, Vasudeva, "the Lord of the World," resumed his own shape as Krishna. He, the Great-Souled One, appearing to Arjuna in the form of grace, consoled His fear-stricken devotee.   50

Arjuna said:

O Granter of All Wishes (Krishna)! As I gaze on Thee again in gentle human shape, my mind is quieted and I feel more like my natural self.   51

The Blessed Lord said:

Very difficult it is to behold, as thou hast done, the Vision Universal! Even the gods ever yearn to see it.   52

But it is not unveiled through one's penance or scriptural lore or gift-giving or formal worship. O Scorcher of the Sense-Foes (Arjuna)! only by undivided devotion (commingling by yoga all thoughts in One Divine Perception) may I be seen as thou hast beheld Me in My Cosmic Form and recognized in reality and finally embraced in Oneness!   53–54

He who works for Me alone, who makes Me his goal, who lovingly surrenders himself to Me, who is nonattached (to My delusive cosmic-dream worlds), who bears ill will toward none (beholding Me in all) — he enters My being, O Arjuna!   55

Aum, Tat, Sat.

In the Upanishad of the holy Bhagavad Gita—the discourse of Lord Krishna to Arjuna, which is the scripture of yoga and the science of God-realization—this is the eleventh chapter, called "The Vision of the Cosmic Form."

CHAPTER XII

Bhakti Yoga: Union Through Devotion

Should the Yogi Worship the Unmanifest, or a Personal God?

Arjuna said:

Those devotees who, ever steadfast, thus worship Thee; and those who adore the Indestructible, the Unmanifested — which of these is better versed in yoga?* 1

The Blessed Lord said:

Those who, fixing their minds on Me, adore Me, ever united to Me with supreme devotion, are in My eyes the perfect knowers of yoga. 2

But those who adore the Indestructible, the Indescribable, the Unmanifested, the All-Pervading, the Incomprehensible, the Immutable, the Unmoving, the Ever-Constant; who have subjugated all of the senses, possess evenmindedness in every circumstance, and devote themselves to the good of all beings — verily, they too attain Me. 3–4

Those whose goal is the Unmanifested increase the difficulties; arduous is the path to the Absolute for embodied beings. 5

But those who venerate Me, giving over all activities to Me (thinking of Me as the Sole Doer), contemplating Me by single-minded yoga — remaining thus absorbed in Me — indeed, O offspring of Pritha (Arjuna), for these whose consciousness is fixed in Me, I become before long their Redeemer to bring them out of the sea of mortal births. 6–7

---

* Here Arjuna refers to the devotee described in the last stanza of the eleventh chapter (he who thinks of God as the Cosmic-Bodied Lord, immanent in all manifestations and who therefore works for Him without personal attachment to anything, without feeling enmity to anyone, enshrining God as his supreme Goal); and to the devotee who worships God as formless or unmanifested Spirit (considering God and Nature as two separate entities). Which devotee is better acquainted with the technique of uniting soul and Spirit?

The Levels of Spiritual Practice and the Stages of Realization

Immerse thy mind in Me alone; concentrate on Me thy discriminative perception; and beyond doubt thou shalt dwell immortally in Me. 8

O Dhananjaya (Arjuna), if thou art not able to keep thy mind wholly on Me, then seek to attain Me by repeated yoga practice. 9

If, again, thou art not able to practice continuous yoga, be thou diligent in performing actions in the thought of Me. Even by engaging in activities on My behalf thou shalt attain supreme divine success. 10

If thou art not able to do even this, then, remaining attached to Me as thy Shelter, relinquish the fruits of all actions while continuing to strive for Self-mastery.* 11

Verily, wisdom (born from yoga practice) is superior to (mechanical) yoga practice; meditation is more desirable than the possession of (theoretical) wisdom; the relinquishment of the fruits of actions is better than (the initial states of) meditation. Renunciation of the fruits of actions is followed immediately by peace. 12

Qualities of the Devotee, Endearing to God

He who is free from hatred toward all creatures, is friendly and kind to all, is devoid of the consciousness of "I-ness" and possessiveness; is evenminded in suffering and joy, forgiving, ever contented; a regular yoga practitioner, constantly trying by yoga to know the Self and to unite with Spirit, possessed of firm determination, with mind and discrimination surrendered to Me — he is My devotee, dear to Me. 13–14

A person who does not disturb the world and who cannot be disturbed by the world, who is free from exultation, jealousy, apprehension, and worry — he too is dear to Me. 15

---

* *Yata-ātma-vān:* lit., "like a mastered self"; that is, emulate those who have attained Self-mastery; keep endeavoring to reach that goal.

He who is free from worldly expectations, who is pure in body and mind, who is ever ready to work, who remains unconcerned with and unafflicted by circumstances, who has forsaken all ego-initiated desireful undertakings — he is My devotee, dear to Me.   16

He who feels neither rejoicing nor loathing toward the glad nor the sad (aspects of phenomenal life), who is free from grief and cravings, who has banished the relative consciousness of good and evil, and who is intently devout — he is dear to Me.   17

He who is tranquil before friend and foe alike, and in encountering adoration and insult, and during the experiences of warmth and chill and of pleasure and suffering; who has relinquished attachment, regarding blame and praise in the same light; who is quiet and easily contented, not attached to domesticity, and of calm disposition and devotional — that person is dear to Me.   18–19

But those who adoringly pursue this undying religion (*dharma*) as heretofore declared, saturated with devotion, supremely engrossed in Me — such devotees are extremely dear to Me.   20

Aum, Tat, Sat.

In the Upanishad of the holy Bhagavad Gita — the discourse of Lord Krishna to Arjuna, which is the scripture of yoga and the science of God-realization — this is the twelfth chapter, called "Bhakti Yoga (Union Through Devotion)."

CHAPTER XIII

The Field and the Knower of the Field

The Divine Forces That Create the Body, the Field Where Good and Evil Are Sown and Reaped

Arjuna said:

O Keshava (Krishna), about Prakriti (intelligent Mother Nature) and Purusha (transcendental God the Father); about *kshetra* ("the field" of the body) and *kshetrajna* (the soul or evolver-cognizer of the bodily field); about knowledge and That which is to be known — this I crave to know. Preface*

The Blessed Lord replied:

O Offspring of Kunti (Arjuna), by the knowers of truth, this body is called *kshetra* ("the field" where good and evil karma is sown and reaped);

"This I crave to know...."

After hearing Krishna's words concerning the union of soul and Spirit through devotion, Arjuna is perplexed as to how the various warring elements of mind (*manas,* or sense consciousness) and discrimination (*buddhi,* or pure divine intelligence) exist within him, and how their clash obstructs divine union. The God-seeking devotee yearns to understand the mystery about outward, matter-bent Cosmic Nature and the inward pull of the transcendental Spirit; and about the sense- and Nature-identified field of the body (*kshetra*) and the Spirit-identified soul (*kshetrajna*). He desires all knowledge about them, and about the Spirit in Its unmanifested state — the supreme object of knowledge.

---

* This prefatory verse is not included in some versions of the Gita. In others it is included and numbered as verse one. More commonly, it is included with no assigned number, so that the traditional total of verses remains at 700, instead of 701.

likewise, that which cognizes the field they call *kshetrajna* (the soul).   1

O Descendant of Bharata (Arjuna), also know Me to be the *Kshetrajna* (Perceiver) in all *kshetras* (the bodies evolved out of the cosmic creative principle and Nature). The understanding of *kshetra* and *kshetrajna* — that is deemed by Me as constituting true wisdom.   2

The True Nature of Matter and Spirit, Body and Soul

Hear from Me briefly about the *kshetra*, its attributes, its cause-and-effect principle, and its distorting influences; and also who He (the *Kshetrajna*) is, and the nature of His powers — truths that have been distinctly celebrated by the *rishis* in many ways: in various chants in the Vedas and in the definitive reasoned analyses of aphorisms about Brahman.   3–4

Succinctly described, the *kshetra* and its modifications are composed of the Unmanifested (Mula-Prakriti, undifferentiated Nature), the five cosmic elements, the ten senses and the one sense mind, intelligence (discrimination), egoism, the five objects of the senses; desire, hate, pleasure, pain, aggregation (the body, a combination of diverse forces), consciousness, and persistence.   5–6

Characteristics of Wisdom

(The sage is marked by) humility, lack of hypocrisy, harmlessness, forgivingness, uprightness, service to the guru, purity of mind and body, steadfastness, self-control;   7

Indifference to sense objects, absence of egotism, understanding of the pain and evils (inherent in mortal life): birth, illness, old age, and death;   8

Nonattachment, nonidentification of the Self with such as one's children, wife, and home; constant equal-mindedness in desirable and undesirable circumstances;   9

Unswerving devotion to Me by the yoga of nonseparativeness, resort to solitary places, avoidance of the company of worldly men;   10

Perseverance in Self-knowledge; and meditative perception of the object of all learning — the true essence or meaning therein. All these qualities constitute wisdom; qualities opposed to them constitute ignorance. 11

Spirit, as Known by the Wise

I will tell you of That which is to be known, because such knowledge bestows immortality. Hear about the beginningless Supreme Spirit — He who is spoken of as neither existent (*sat*) nor nonexistent (*asat*). 12

He dwells in the world, enveloping all — everywhere, His hands and feet; present on all sides, His eyes and ears, His mouths and heads; 13

Shining in all the sense faculties, yet transcending the senses; unattached to creation, yet the Mainstay of all; free from the *gunas* (modes of Nature), yet the Enjoyer of them. 14

He is within and without all that exists, the animate and the inanimate; near He is, and far; imperceptible because of His subtlety. 15

He, the Indivisible One, appears as countless beings; He maintains and destroys those forms, then creates them anew. 16

The Light of All Lights, beyond darkness; Knowledge itself, That which is to be known, the Goal of all learning, He is seated in the hearts of all. 17

I have briefly described the Field, the nature of wisdom, and the Object of wisdom. Understanding these, My devotee enters My being. 18

Purusha and Prakriti (Spirit and Nature)

Know that both Purusha and Prakriti are beginningless; and know also that all modifications and qualities (*gunas*) are born of Prakriti. 19

In the creation of the effect (the body) and the instrument (the senses), Prakriti is spoken of as the cause; in the experience of joy and sorrow, Purusha is said to be the cause. 20

Purusha involved with Prakriti experiences the *gunas* born of Nature. Attachment to the three qualities of Prakriti causes the soul to take embodiment in good and evil wombs.   21

The Supreme Spirit, transcendent and existing in the body, is the detached Beholder, the Consenter, the Sustainer, the Experiencer, the Great Lord, and also the Highest Self.   22

Whatever his mode of life, he who thus realizes Purusha and the threefold nature of Prakriti will not again suffer rebirth.   23

To behold the Self in the self (purified ego) by the self (illumined mind), some men follow the path of meditation, some the path of knowledge, and some the path of selfless action.   24

Some men, ignorant of the three main roads, listen to the instructions of the guru. Following the path of worship, regarding the ancient teachings as the Highest Refuge, such men also attain immortality.   25

Verse 34:
Opening the Eye of Wisdom Through Yoga

When by the right method of yoga, divine union, the devotee's all-seeing spiritual eye of wisdom is opened in *samadhi* meditation, the cumulative knowledge of truth becomes realization — intuitive perception or oneness with Reality.

Through this eye of omniscience, the yogi beholds the comings and goings of beings and universes as the workings of the relativities of Prakriti's illusory *maya* superimposed on the singular cosmic consciousness of Spirit. By dissolving successively in the light of the "One Sun" of Cosmic Consciousness the evolutes of Prakriti from matter to Spirit, the yogi is liberated from all trammels and misconceptions of cosmic delusion.

Identified with the pure immutable *Kshetrajna* (the Evolver-Cognizer of Nature and its domain of matter), the liberated soul can at will consciously dream with Prakriti the metamorphoses of consciousness into "the field" of matter, *kshetra,* or by choice remain wholly awake in Spirit, free from all nightmares inherent in *maya's* realm of clashing opposites.

Liberation: Differentiating Between the Field and Its Knower

O Best of the Bharatas (Arjuna), whatever exists — every being, every object; the animate, the inanimate — understand that to be born from the union of *Kshetra* and *Kshetrajna* (Nature and Spirit). 26

He sees truly who perceives the Supreme Lord present equally in all creatures, the Imperishable amidst the perishing. 27

He who is conscious of the omnipresence of God does not injure the Self by the self. That man reaches the Supreme Goal. 28

He who sees that all actions are performed in their entirety by Prakriti alone, and not by the Self, is indeed a beholder of truth. 29

When a man beholds all separate beings as existent in the One that has expanded Itself into the many, he then merges with Brahman. 30

O Son of Kunti (Arjuna), whereas this Supreme Self, the Unchanging, is beginningless and free from attributes, It neither performs actions nor is affected by them, even though dwelling in the body. 31

As the all-pervading ether, because of its subtlety, is beyond taint, similarly the Self, though seated everywhere in the body, is ever taintless. 32

O Bharata (Arjuna), as the one sun illumines the entire world, so does the Lord of the Field (God and His reflection as the soul) illumine the whole field (Nature and the bodily "little nature"). 33

They enter the Supreme who perceive with the eye of wisdom the distinction between the *Kshetra* and the *Kshetrajna* and who also perceive the method of liberation of beings from Prakriti. 34

Aum, Tat, Sat.

In the Upanishad of the holy Bhagavad Gita — the discourse of Lord Krishna to Arjuna, which is the scripture of yoga and the science of God-realization — this is the thirteenth chapter, called "Union Through Discriminating Between the Field and the Knower of the Field."

CHAPTER XIV

Transcending the Gunas

The Three Qualities (Gunas) Inherent
in Cosmic Nature

The Blessed Lord said:

Again I shall speak about that highest wisdom which transcends all knowledge. With this wisdom all sages at the end of life have attained the final Perfection. 1

Embracing this wisdom, established in my Being, sages are not reborn even at the start of a new cycle of creation, nor are they troubled at the time of universal dissolution. 2

My womb is the Great Prakriti (Mahat-Brahma) into which I deposit the seed (of My Intelligence); this is the cause of the birth of all beings. 3

O Son of Kunti (Arjuna), of all forms — produced from whatsoever wombs — Great Prakriti is their original womb (Mother), and I am the seed-imparting Father. 4

O Mighty-armed (Arjuna)! the *gunas* inherent in Prakriti—*sattva, rajas,* and *tamas*—imprison in the body the Imperishable Dweller. 5

O Sinless One (Arjuna)! of these three *gunas,* the stainless *sattva* gives enlightenment and health. Nevertheless, it binds man through attachment to happiness and attachment to knowledge. 6

O Son of Kunti (Arjuna), understand that the activating *rajas* is imbued with passion, giving birth to desire and attachment; it strongly binds the embodied soul by a clinging to works. 7

O Bharata (Arjuna)! know that *tamas* arises from ignorance, deluding all embodied beings. It binds them by misconception, idleness, and slumber. 8

Sattva attaches one to happiness; *rajas* to activity; and *tamas*, by eclipsing the power of discrimination, to miscomprehension.   9

Mixture of Good and Evil in Human Nature

Sometimes *sattva* is predominant, overpowering *rajas* and *tamas;* sometimes *rajas* prevails, not *sattva* or *tamas;* and sometimes *tamas* obscures *sattva* and *rajas*.   10

One may know that *sattva* is prevalent when the light of wisdom shines through all the sense gates of the body.   11

Preponderance of *rajas* causes greed, activity, undertaking of works, restlessness, and desire.   12

Tamas as the ruling guna produces darkness, sloth, neglect of duties, and delusion.   13

A man who dies with *sattva* qualities predominant rises to the taintless regions in which dwell knowers of the Highest.   14

When *rajas* prevails at the time of death, a person is reborn among those attached to activity. He who dies permeated with *tamas* enters the wombs (environment, family, state of existence) of the deeply deluded.   15

It is said (by the sages) that the fruit of sattvic actions is harmony and purity. The fruit of rajasic actions is pain. The fruit of tamasic actions is ignorance.   16

Wisdom arises from *sattva;* greed from *rajas;* and heedlessness, delusion, and ignorance from *tamas*.   17

Those established in *sattva* go upward; the rajasic dwell in the middle; those men descend who are engrossed in the lowest *guna* — *tamas*.   18

The Nature of the Jivanmukta — One Who Rises Above Nature's Qualities

When the seer perceives (in creation) no agent except the three modes, and cognizes That which is higher than the *gunas*, he enters My Being.   19

Having transcended the three modes of Nature — the cause of physical embodiment — a man is released from the sufferings of birth, old age, and death; he attains immortality.   20

Arjuna said:

O Lord, what signs distinguish the man who has transcended the three modes? What is his behavior? How does he rise beyond the triple qualities?   21

The Blessed Lord said:

O Pandava (Arjuna), he who does not abhor the presence of the *gunas* — illumination, activity, and ignorance — nor deplore their absence;   22

Remaining like one unconcerned, undisturbed by the three modes — realizing that they alone are operating throughout creation; not oscillating in mind but ever Self-centered;   23

Unaffected by joy and sorrow, praise and blame — secure in his divine nature; regarding with an equal eye a clod of clay, a stone, and gold; the same in his attitude toward pleasant or unpleasant (men and experiences); firm-minded;   24

Uninfluenced by respect or insult; treating friend and enemy alike; abandoning all delusions of personal doership — he it is who has transcended the triple qualities!   25

He who serves Me with undeviating devotion transcends the *gunas* and is qualified to become Brahman.   26

For I am the basis of the Infinite, the Immortal, the Indestructible; and of eternal Dharma and unalloyed Bliss.   27

Aum, Tat, Sat.

In the Upanishad of the holy Bhagavad Gita — the discourse of Lord Krishna to Arjuna, which is the scripture of yoga and the science of God-realization — this is the fourteenth chapter, called "Union Through Transcending Nature's Three Qualities."

CHAPTER XV

Purushottama: The Uttermost Being

Eternal Ashvattha: The Tree of Life

The Blessed Lord said:

They (the wise) speak of an eternal *ashvattha* tree, with roots above and boughs beneath, whose leaves are Vedic hymns. He who understands this tree of life is a Veda-knower. 1

Its branches spread above and below, nurtured by the *gunas;* its buds are the sense objects; and downward, into the world of men, extend the rootlings that force man to actions. 2

The true nature of this tree, its beginning, its end, and its modes of continuity—none of these are understood by ordinary men. The wise, having destroyed the firmly rooted *ashvattha* with the powerful axe of non-attachment; thinking, "I take refuge in the Primeval Purusha from whom alone issued the immemorial processes of creation," seek the Supreme Goal. Reaching It, they return to phenomenal existence no more. 3–4

The Abode of the Unmanifest

Without craving for honor, free from delusion and malignant attachment, all longings banished, disengaged from the pair of opposites — pleasure and pain — ever established in the Self, the undeceived attain the immutable state. 5

Where no sun or moon or fire shines, that is My Supreme Abode. Having reached there, men are never reborn. 6

How Spirit Manifests as the Soul

An eternal part of Myself, manifesting as a living soul in the world of beings, attracts to itself the six senses, including the mind, which rest in Prakriti. 7

When the Lord as the *jiva* acquires a body, He brings with Him the mind and the senses. When He leaves that body, He takes them and goes, even as the wind wafts away scents from their dwelling places (in flowers).   8

Presiding over the mind and the senses of hearing, sight, touch, taste, and smell, He enjoys the sensory world.   9

The deluded do not perceive Him staying or departing or experiencing the world of the *gunas*. Those whose eye of wisdom is open see Him.   10

The yogis striving for liberation see Him existing in themselves; but those who are unpurified and undisciplined are unable to perceive Him even when they struggle to do so.   11

The light of the sun that illumines the whole world, the light from the moon, and the light in fire — know this radiance to be Mine.   12

Permeating earth with My effulgence, I support all beings; having become the watery moon, I bring forth all plant forms.   13

Having become *Vaishvanara* (fiery power), I exist in the body of living creatures; and, acting through *prana* and *apana*, I digest food that is eaten in four ways.   14

Also, I am seated in the heart of all beings; and from Me come memory and knowledge, as well as their loss. Verily I am That which is to be known through the Vedas; indeed, I am the Veda-Knower and the Author of the *Vedanta*.   15

The Supreme Spirit: Beyond the Perishable and the Imperishable

There are two Beings (Purushas) in the cosmos, the destructible and the indestructible. The creatures are the destructible, the *Kutastha* is the indestructible.   16

But there exists Another, the Highest Being, designated the "Supreme Spirit" — the Eternal Lord who, permeating the three worlds, upholds them.   17

I (the Lord) am beyond the perishable (Prakriti) and am also higher than the imperishable (*Kutastha*). Therefore, in the worlds and in the Veda (the intuitive perception of undeluded souls) I am proclaimed Purushottama, the Uttermost Being. 18

Whosoever, freed from delusion, knows Me thus as the Supreme Spirit, knows all, O Descendant of Bharata (Arjuna). He worships Me with his whole being. 19

Herewith, O Sinless One (Arjuna), have I taught thee this most profound wisdom. Understanding it, a man becomes a sage, one who has successfully fulfilled all his duties, and yet continues in dutiful actions. 20

Aum, Tat, Sat.

In the Upanishad of the holy Bhagavad Gita — the discourse of Lord Krishna to Arjuna, which is the scripture of yoga and the science of God-realization — this is the fifteenth chapter, called "Union With the Supreme Spirit."

CHAPTER XVI

Embracing the Divine and
Shunning the Demonic

The Soul Qualities That Make Man Godlike

The Blessed Lord said:

Fearlessness, purity of heart, perseverance in acquiring wisdom and in practicing yoga, charity, subjugation of the senses, performance of holy rites, study of the scriptures, self-discipline, straightforwardness;   1

Noninjury, truthfulness, freedom from wrath, renunciation, peacefulness, nonslanderousness, compassion for all creatures, absence of greed, gentleness, modesty, lack of restlessness;   2

Radiance of character, forgiveness, patience, cleanness, freedom from hate, absence of conceit — these qualities are the wealth of a divinely inclined person, O Descendant of Bharata.   3

The Nature and Fate of Souls Who Shun the Divine

Vainglorious pride, arrogance, conceit, wrath, harshness, and ignorance mark the man who is born with the demonic nature, O Son of Pritha (Arjuna).   4

The divine qualities bestow liberation; the demonic qualities lead to bondage. Fear not, O Pandava (Arjuna)! thou art endowed with the divine traits.   5

Two types of men exist in this world: the divine and the demonic. I have told you fully about the divine qualities; now hear about the demonic, O Son of Pritha (Arjuna).   6

The demonic know not the right path of action or when to refrain from action. They lack purity and truth and proper conduct.　　　7

They say: "The world has no moral foundation, no abiding truth, no God or Ruler; produced not by a systematic causal order, its sole purpose is lustful desire — what else?"　　　8

With their feeble intellects, such ruined men cling to their erroneous beliefs and commit many atrocities. They are enemies of the world, bent on its destruction.　　　9

Abandoned to insatiable longings, full of dissimulation, self-conceit, and insolence, possessing evil ideas through delusion, all their actions are impurely motivated.　　　10

Believing that fulfillment of bodily desires is man's highest aim, confident that this world is "all," such persons are engrossed till the moment of death in earthly cares and concerns.　　　11

Bound by hundreds of fetters of selfish hopes and expectations, enslaved by wrath and passion, they strive to provide for physical enjoyments by amassing wealth dishonestly.　　　12

"This I have acquired today; now another desire I shall satisfy. This is my present wealth; however, more shall also be mine.　　　13

"I have killed this enemy; and the others also I will slay. I am the ruler among men; I enjoy all possessions; I am successful, strong, and happy.　　　14

"I am rich and well-born; can any other be compared with me? Ostentatiously I will give alms and make formal sacrifices; I will rejoice." Thus they speak, led astray by lack of wisdom.　　　15

Harboring bewildering thoughts, caught in the net of delusion, craving only sensual delights, they sink into a foul hell.　　　16

Vain, stubborn, intoxicated by pride in wealth, they perform the sacrifices hypocritically and without following the scriptural injunctions.　　　17

Egotistical, forceful, haughty, lascivious, and prone to rage, these malicious men despise Me who dwells within them and within all other men.　　　18

These cruel and hating perpetrators of evil, worst among men, I hurl again and again into demonic wombs in the spheres of transmigration.   19

Entering the state of existence of the *asuras*, deluded birth after birth, failing to attain Me, they thus descend to the very lowest depths.   20

Lust, anger, and greed — these constitute the threefold gate of hell leading to the destruction of the soul's welfare. These three, therefore, man should abandon.   21

O Son of Kunti (Arjuna)! By turning away from these three entrances to the realm of darkness, man behaves according to his own highest good and thereafter reaches the Supreme.   22

The Right Understanding of Scriptural Guidance for the Conduct of Life

He who ignores the scriptural commands and who follows his own foolish desires does not find happiness or perfection or the Infinite Goal.   23

Therefore, take the scriptures as your guide in determining what should be done and what should be avoided. With intuitive understanding of the injunctions declared in holy writ, be pleased to perform thy duties here.   24

Aum, Tat, Sat.

In the Upanishad of the holy Bhagavad Gita — the discourse of Lord Krishna to Arjuna, which is the scripture of yoga and the science of God-realization — this is the sixteenth chapter, called "Union Through Embracing the Divine and Shunning the Demonic."

CHAPTER XVII

Three Kinds of Faith

Three Patterns of Worship

Arjuna said:

Those who set aside the scriptural rules but who perform sacrifices with devotion — what is their status, O Krishna? Are they of sattvic, rajasic, or tamasic nature? 1

The Blessed Lord said:

The natural faith of the embodied is threefold — sattvic, rajasic, and tamasic. Hear thou about it. 2

The devotion of each man is in agreement with his inborn nature. His inclination is the pattern of his being; whatever his faith is, that verily is he. 3

The sattvic pay homage to the Devas, the rajasic to the Yakshas and the Rakshasas, and the tamasic to the Pretas and the hosts of Bhutas. 4

Know those men to be of asuric nature who perform terrible austerities not authorized by the scriptures. Hypocrites, egotists — possessed by lust, attachment, and power madness — senselessly they torture the bodily elements and also offend Me, the Indweller. 5–6

Three Classes of Food

Each of the three classes of men even likes one of the three kinds of food; so also their *yajnas*, penances, and almsgivings. Hear thou about these distinctions. 7

Foods that promote longevity, vitality, endurance, health, cheerfulness, and good appetite; and that are savory, mild, substantial, and agreeable to the body, are liked by pure-minded (sattvic) persons. 8

Foods that are bitter, sour, saltish, excessively hot, pungent, harsh, and burning are preferred by rajasic men; and produce pain, sorrow, and disease.   9

Foods that are nutritionally worthless, insipid, putrid, stale, refuse, and impure are enjoyed by tamasic persons.   10

Three Grades of Spiritual Practices

That *yajna* (sacrifice or performance of duty) is sattvic which is offered by men who desire no fruit of the action; and which is done in accordance with the scriptures, for the sake of righteousness only.   11

Know thou, O Best of the Bharatas (Arjuna)! that the *yajna* performed in the hope of reward and in an ostentatious spirit is rajasic in nature.   12

That *yajna* is condemned as tamasic which is without regard for the scriptural injunctions, without offerings of food and gifts of appreciation,* without sacred prayers or chants, and without devotion (to God).   13

Veneration of the Devas, the twice-born, the gurus, and the wise; purity, straightforwardness, continence, and nonviolence are considered the penance or austerity of the body.   14

Meditative communion with one's own true Self, and uttering words that cause no agitation and that are truthful, pleasant, and beneficial, are called the austerity of speech.   15

A calm and contented mental clarity, kindliness, silence, self-control, and purity of character constitute the austerity of the mind.   16

This threefold penance, sattvic in its nature, is practiced by persevering men possessing great devotion who desire no fruit of actions.   17

---

* A part of the tradition of a sanctified *yajna,* or formal worship, is distribution of food (*srishta anna*) and a gift of appreciation (*dakshina*) to the guru or presiding officiant. The offering of food to guests, the poor, or "Brahmins" (priests, renunciants, or other holy persons who have given their lives to serving God) symbolizes a charitable heart that shares its blessings, which is man's duty to his fellow beings. The spiritually obligatory "fee" or donation offered to the guru or officiating priest expresses the gratitude owed to the one from whom spiritual ministration has been received, and recognition of the value of that instruction.

Austerities are said to be rajasic, unstable and fleeting, when practiced for the purpose of ostentation and for gaining men's recognition, honor, and homage. 18

Tamasic austerities are those based on ignorance or foolishness or performed for self-torture or for injuring others. 19

Three Kinds of Giving

The good or sattvic gift is one made for the sake of righteousness, without expectation of anything in return, and is bestowed in proper time and place on a deserving person. 20

That gift is deemed rajasic which is offered with reluctance or in the thought of receiving a return or of gaining merit. 21

A tamasic gift is one bestowed at a wrong time and place, on an unworthy person, contemptuously or without goodwill. 22

Aum-Tat-Sat: God the Father, Son, and Holy Ghost

"*Aum-Tat-Sat*" is considered to be the triple designation of Brahman (God). By this power were created, in the beginning, the Brahmins (knowers of Brahman), the Vedas, and the sacrificial rites. 23

Therefore the acts of the followers of Brahman — sacrifice, gift-giving, and austerities as enjoined by the scriptures — are always started with the chanting of "*Aum.*" 24

The seekers of liberation then perform the various rites of sacrifice, gift-giving, and austerities while concentrating on "*Tat*" without desiring results. 25

The word "*Sat*" is the designation of the Supreme Reality (beyond creation) and of goodness (emanating from It in all creation). "*Sat*" also refers to the higher forms of spiritual action. 26

The state of stability in the higher rites of sacrifice, self-discipline, and devotional offering is spoken of as "*Sat*" (communion with God as transcendent Cosmic Consciousness). Indeed, the same spiritual action connected with "*Tat*" (realization of God as immanent in creation) is also called "*Sat.*"   27

O Partha (Arjuna)! Whatever sacrifice is offered, gift bestowed, or austerity performed without faith (devotion) is called "*asat.*" It is worthless here and in the hereafter.   28

Aum, Tat, Sat.

In the Upanishad of the holy Bhagavad Gita — the discourse of Lord Krishna to Arjuna, which is the scripture of yoga and the science of God-realization — this is the seventeenth chapter, called "Union Through the Three Kinds of Faith."

CHAPTER XVIII

"In Truth Do I Promise Thee:
Thou Shalt Attain Me"

Renunciation: The Divine Art of Acting in the World With Unselfishness and Nonattachment

Arjuna said:

O Hrishikesha, O Mighty-Armed, O Slayer of (the demon) Keshi! I desire to know the true meaning of *sannyasa* (renunciation) and also of *tyaga* (relinquishment), and the distinction between them.   1

The Blessed Lord said:

Sages call "*sannyasa*" the renunciation of all actions done with desire. The wise declare that "*tyaga*" is the renunciation of the fruits of activities.   2

Some philosophers say that all work should be forsaken as full of taint. Others declare that the activities of *yajna* (holy fire rite), *dana* (philanthropy), and *tapas* (self-discipline) ought not to be abandoned.   3

Consequently, understand from Me the ultimate truth about renunciation, O Best of the Bharatas (Arjuna). For renunciation has been spoken of as consisting of three kinds, O Tiger among Men.   4

The action involved in *yajna, dana,* and *tapas* verily ought to be performed, and should not be forsaken, for the holy fire rite, philanthropy, and self-discipline sanctify the wise.   5

But even these activities ought to be performed, O Partha (Arjuna), forsaking attachment to them and the desire for their fruits. This is My supreme and sure conviction.   6

The relinquishment of dutiful action is improper. Renunciation of such action through delusion is spoken of as tamasic (evil).   7

He who relinquishes action as being intrinsically difficult, for fear of painful trouble to the body, is performing rajasic renunciation. He is unable to attain the reward of renunciation.   8

O Arjuna, when dutiful action is performed solely because it should be done, forsaking attachment to it and its fruit, that renunciation is considered sattvic.   9

The renunciant absorbed in *sattva,* with a calm understanding, free from doubts, neither abhors unpleasant action nor delights in a pleasant one.   10

It is truly impossible for an embodied being to abandon actions completely, but he who relinquishes the fruit of action is called a renunciant.   11

The triune fruit of action — good, harmful, and mixed — springs up in nonrenunciants after their demise, but in renunciants never.   12

The Roots of Action and the Consummation of Action (Liberation)

O Mighty-armed (Arjuna), learn from Me the five causes for the performance of all action, which are chronicled in the highest wisdom (Sankhya) wherein all action terminates.   13

The human body; the pseudoagent there; the manifold instrumentality (senses, mind, and intelligence); the various divergent functions; and, lastly, the fifth of these, the presiding deity, destiny: 14

These five are the causes of all actions — either right or wrong — performed by man through his body, speech, and mind.   15

This being the case, whoever of perverted consciousness views through a nonclarified understanding the Self as the exclusive disposer of action, he sees not.   16

He who is above the obsession of egoism, whose intelligence is unadulterated, though he slay these people (ready for battle at Kurukshetra), he slays not; neither is he bound by such act.   17

The knower, the knowledge, and the known constitute the triune stimulus to action. The agent, the instrument, and the activity are the threefold basis of action.   18

Three Grades of Knowledge, Action, and Character

Knowledge, action, and agent in the Sankhya philosophy are described as being of but three kinds, according to the distinction of the three *gunas*. Please hear duly about these also.   19

O Arjuna, understand that knowledge to be sattvic by which the one indestructible Spirit is perceived in all beings, undivided in the divided.   20

But that knowledge which perceives in the aggregate world of beings manifold entities of different varieties, distinct from one another — understand that knowledge to be rajasic.   21

And that knowledge which concentrates on a single effect as if it were the whole, disregarding motive, lacking conformance with the principles of truth — trivial and easy — is declared to be tamasic.   22

That action which is divinely directed, which is performed in a state of complete nonattachment, without attraction or repulsion and without desiring the fruits of action, is said to be sattvic.   23

Action that is inspired by longing for satisfaction of desires, or performed with egotism and colossal effort, is said to be rajasic.   24

Tamasic action is that which is instituted through delusion, without measuring one's ability, and disregarding the consequences — loss to oneself of health, wealth, and influence; and harm to others.   25

That agent who is without egotism or attachment, untouched by fulfillment or unfulfillment, and endowed with courage and zeal, is called sattvic.   26

That instrument of action, or agent, who is full of attachment, full of longing for the fruits of action, full of greed, impurity, and ruthless propensities; who becomes easily jubilant or depressed, is called rajasic.   27

An agent who is oscillating in body and mind, conscienceless, ar-

rogant, unscrupulous, malicious, slothful, grieving, and procrastinat-
ing is tamasic.   28

Intelligence (*buddhi*), Fortitude (*dhriti*), and Happiness (*sukham*): Their Higher and Lower Expressions

O Winner of Wealth (Arjuna), I will explain, separately and exhaustively, the threefold distinctions of intelligence and fortitude according to the *gunas*. Please listen.   29

That intellect is sattvic, O Partha (Arjuna), which correctly understands the paths of desireful action and renunciation, undutiful and
dutiful actions, as the causes of apprehension and fearlessness, bondage and salvation.   30

O Partha (Arjuna), that intellect is rajasic by which one perceives
in a grossly distorted manner righteousness (*dharma*) and unrighteous-
ness (*adharma*), dutiful action and undutiful action.   31

O Partha (Arjuna), that intellect is tamasic which, being enveloped
in gloom, considers irreligion as religion, and looks upon all things in
a perverted way.   32

The resolute constancy by which one regulates the functions of the
mind, *prana*, and senses — by restraining their prostitution (wayward
oscillation) through yoga practice — that fortitude (*dhriti*) is sattvic,
O Partha (Arjuna).   33

The resolute inner patience that causes one to regulate his mind to
dharma (religious duty), desire, and riches — while longing for the fruits
thereof, because of attachment — that, O Partha (Arjuna), is *rajasic-
dhriti*.   34

That by which a stupid man does not forsake over-sleep, fear,
sorrow, despair, and wanton conceit, O Partha (Arjuna), is *tamasic-
dhriti*.   35

O Stubborn Bull of Realization (Arjuna)! Pray hear from Me
now about the three kinds of happiness: Transcendent happiness (supreme bliss), gained by repeated recollection of the mind,* and in

---

* *Abhyāsād ramate*: from *abhyāsa*, lit., "the continuous effort to hold the mind in its pure sattvic

which one knows the extinguishment of all pain;   36

That which is born of the clear perceptive discrimination of Self-realization — that happiness is called sattvic. It seems like poison at first, but like nectar afterward.   37

That happiness which springs from the conjunction of the senses and matter is termed rajasic. It seems like nectar in the beginning and like poison in the end.   38

That elusive happiness which originates and ends in self-delusion, stemming from over-sleep, slothfulness, and miscomprehension, is called tamasic.   39

Discerning One's Divinely Ordained Duty in Life

There is no being in the world, or again among the deities in the astral heaven, who is free from these three qualities, born of Prakriti (Cosmic Nature, created by God).   40

O Scorcher of Foes (Arjuna)! The duties of Brahmins, of Kshatriyas, of Vaishyas, as also of Sudras, are allocated according to the *gunas* (qualities) springing from their own nature.   41

Mind control, sense control, self-discipline, purity, forgiveness, honesty, wisdom, Self-realization, and faith in a hereafter constitute the duties of Brahmins, springing from their own nature.   42

Valor, radiance, resolute endurance, skillfulness, not fleeing from battle, munificence, and leadership are the natural duties of the Kshatriyas.   43

Tilling the soil, cattle breeding, and business are the natural duties of the Vaishyas. Actions that are of service to others are the natural duty of the Sudras.   44

Each one attentive to his own duty, man gains the highest success. How, devoted to his inborn duty, he attains success — that hear.   45

A man attains perfection by worshiping, with his natural gifts,

---

state"; and from *ram*, lit., "to enjoy," "to still; set at rest" — that is, to gain transcendent happiness. When the mind is recollected in its pure sattvic state, the sensory tumult is stilled and the transcendent supreme bliss of the soul becomes manifest.

Him from whom all beings are evolved, and by whom all this world is permeated.   46

Better than the well-accomplished *dharma* (duty) of another is one's own *dharma*, even though lacking merit (somewhat imperfect). He who performs the duty decreed by his inborn nature contracts no sin.   47

O Offspring of Kunti (Arjuna), one should not abandon one's in-born duty, even though it has some imperfection, for all undertakings are marred by blemishes, as flame by smoke.   48

Summary of the Gita's Message: How God-realization Is Attained

That individual gains uttermost perfection — the actionless state of realization through renunciation — who keeps his intellect ever detached from worldly ties and passions,* who is victorious in regaining his soul, and who is without desires.   49

O Son of Kunti (Arjuna), hear from Me, in brief, how he who gains such perfection finds Brahman, the supreme culmination of wisdom.   50

Absorbed in a completely purified intellect, subjugating the body and the senses by resolute patience, forsaking (as much as possible) sound and all other sense entanglements, relinquishing attachment and repulsion;   51

Remaining in a sequestered place, eating lightly, controlling body, speech, and mind; ever absorbed in divine meditation and in soul-uniting yoga; possessing dispassion;   52

Peaceful, renouncing egotism, power, vanity, lust, anger, posses-sions, and the "me and mine" consciousness — he is qualified to be-come one with Brahman.   53

By becoming engrossed in Brahman — calm-souled, neither la-

---

* *Asaktabuddhi:* lit., "...who keeps his intellect ever detached." *Buddhi,* the discriminating fac-ulty of the soul, when pure and undistorted by the influence of *manas,* the sense mind, is truth-revealing, drawing the consciousness to its native state in the true Self, the soul.

menting nor craving; beholding equality in all beings — he gains supreme devotion toward Me.   54

By that supreme devotion he realizes Me and My nature — what
and who I am; after knowing these truths, he quickly makes his entry
into Me.   55

Over and above performing faithfully all one's duties, taking shelter in Me, it is by My pleasure a devotee obtains the eternal, unchangeable state.   56

Mentally dedicating all actions to Me, considering Me as the
Supreme Goal, employing *buddhi-yoga* (union through discriminative
wisdom), continuously absorb thy heart in Me.   57

With heart absorbed in Me, and by My grace, thou shalt overcome
all impediments; but if through egotism thou wilt not heed Me, thou
shalt meet destruction.   58

If, clinging to the ego, thou sayest: "I will not battle," fruitless is thy
resolution! Prakriti, thine inborn nature, will force thee to fight.   59

O Offspring of Kunti (Arjuna), shackled by thine own karma, inborn in thy nature, what through delusion thou wouldst not do, thou
wilt helplessly be compelled to do.   60

O Arjuna, the Lord is lodged in the hearts of all creatures, and by
His cosmic delusion (*maya*) compels all beings to rotate as if attached
to a machine.   61

O Descendant of Bharata (Arjuna), take shelter in Him with all the
eagerness of thy heart. By His grace thou shalt obtain the utmost peace
and the Eternal Shelter.   62

Thus hath wisdom, most secret of all secrets, been given to thee by
Me. After exhaustively reflecting about it, act as thou desirest.   63

Again listen to My supreme word, the most secret of all. Because thou
art dearly loved by Me, I will relate what is beneficial to thee.   64

Absorb thy mind in Me; become My devotee; resign all things to
Me; bow down to Me. Thou art dear to Me, so in truth do I promise
thee: Thou shalt attain Me!   65

Forsaking all other *dharmas* (duties), remember Me alone;* I will free thee from all sins (accruing from nonperformance of those lesser duties). Do not grieve!   66

Never voice these truths to one who is without self-control or devotion, nor to one who performs no service or does not care to hear, nor to one who speaks ill of Me.   67

Whosoever shall impart to My devotees the supreme secret knowledge, with utmost devotion to Me, shall without doubt come unto Me. Not any among men performs more priceless service to Me than he; in all the world there shall be none dearer to Me.   68–69

He who studies and knows (intuitively perceives) this sacred dialogue between us will be worshiping Me by the sacrifice (*yajna*) of wisdom. Such is My holy utterance.   70

Even that individual — full of devotion and devoid of scorn — who merely listens to and heeds this sacred dialogue, being freed from earthly karma, shall dwell in the blessed worlds of the virtuous.   71

The Dialogue Between Spirit and Soul Concludes

O Partha (Arjuna), hast thou listened to this wisdom with concentrated heart? O Dhananjaya, hast thy delusion-born ignorance been annihilated?   72

Arjuna said:

My delusion is gone! I have regained memory (of my soul) through Thy grace, O Achyuta (matchless Krishna). I am firmly established; my dubiousness has vanished. I will act according to Thy word.   73

Sanjaya said:

Thus have I listened to this wondrous discourse between Vasudeva (Krishna) and the high-souled Partha (Arjuna), causing the hair on my body to stand on end in a thrill of joy.   74

---

* *Mām ekaṁ śaraṇaṁ vraja:* lit., "Become (*vraja*) sheltered (*śaraṇaṁ*, 'protected'—from delusion) in oneness (*ekaṁ*) with Me (*mām*)." "Always keep your consciousness in My sheltering Presence"; i.e., "Remember Me alone."

Through the grace of Vyasa, this supreme secret Yoga has been bestowed on me, manifested to my consciousness directly by Krishna himself, the Lord of Yoga! 75

O King Dhritarashtra, as I recall and recall the extraordinary and sacred dialogue between Keshava (Krishna) and Arjuna, I am over-joyed again and again. 76

And, O King Dhritarashtra, as I recall and recall again the colossal manifestation* of Hari (Krishna), great is my amazement; I am ever renewed in joy. 77

Such is my faith: that, wherever is manifest the Lord of Yoga, Krishna; and wherever is present Partha (Arjuna, a true devotee), expert wielder of the bow of self-control, there too are success, victory, attainment of powers, and the unfailing law of self-discipline (which leads to liberation). 78

Aum, Tat, Sat.

In the Upanishad of the holy Bhagavad Gita — the discourse of Lord Krishna to Arjuna, which is the scripture of yoga and the science of God-realization — this is the eighteenth chapter, called "Union Through Renunciation and Liberation."

---

* *Vishvarupa*, the cosmic form.

Conclusion

"Arise! Before you is the royal path!"

The words of Lord Krishna to Arjuna in the Bhagavad Gita are at once a profound scripture on the science of yoga, union with God, and a textbook for everyday living. The student is led step by step with Arjuna from the mortal consciousness of spiritual doubt and weakheartedness to divine attunement and inner resolve. The timeless and universal message of the Gita is all-encompassing in its expression of truth. The Gita teaches man his rightful duty in life, and how to discharge it with the dispassion that avoids pain and nurtures wisdom and success. The enigmas of creation are resolved in an understanding of the nature of matter. The mysteries that veil the Infinite Spirit are sundered one by one to reveal a beloved God whose awesome omnipotence is tempered with a tender love and compassion that readily responds to a sincere call from His devotees.

In summation, the sublime essence of the Bhagavad Gita is that right action, nonattachment to the world and to its sense pleasures, and union with God by the highest yoga of *pranayama* meditation, learned from an enlightened guru, constitute the royal path to God-attainment.

The *Kriya Yoga* technique, taught by Krishna to Arjuna and referred to in Gita chapters IV:29 and V:27–28, is the supreme spiritual science of yoga meditation. Secreted during the materialistic ages, this indestructible yoga was revived for modern man by Mahavatar Babaji and taught by the Gurus of Self-Realization Fellowship/Yogoda Satsanga Society of India. Babaji himself ordained me to spread this holy science of God-union. Through the blessings of Bhagavan Krishna and Mahavatar Babaji, whom I behold in Spirit as one, and of my guru and *paramguru*, Swami Sri Yukteswar and Lahiri Mahasaya, I offer to the world this interpretation of the Gita as it has been divinely revealed to me. Any devotee who will emulate Arjuna—epitome of the ideal disciple—and perform his rightful duty with nonattachment, and perfect his practice of yoga meditation through a technique such as *Kriya Yoga,* will similarly draw the blessings and guidance of God and win the victory of Self-realization.

As God talked with Arjuna, so will He talk with you. As He lifted up the spirit and consciousness of Arjuna, so will He uplift you. As He granted Arjuna supreme spiritual vision, so will He confer enlightenment on you.

We have seen in the Bhagavad Gita the story of the soul's journey back to God—a journey each one must make. O divine soul! like Arjuna, "Forsake this small weakheartedness (of mortal consciousness). Arise!" Before you is the royal path.

SANSKRIT EPITHETS OF LORD KRISHNA AND ARJUNA IN THE BHAGAVAD GITA

Lord Krishna:

Achyuta — Changeless One; Matchless One

Anantarupa — One of Inexhaustible Form

Aprameya — Illimitable One

Apratimaprabhava — Lord of Power Incomparable

Arisudana — Destroyer of Foes

Bhagavan — Blessed Lord

Deva — Lord

Devesha — Lord of Gods

Govinda — Chief Herdsman; presiding over and controlling the "cows" of the senses

Hari — "Stealer" of hearts

Hrishikesha — Lord of the Senses

Isham Idyam — Adorable One

Jagannivasa — Cosmic Guardian (Shelter of the World)

Janardana — Granter of Man's Prayers

Kamalapattraksha — Lotus-eyed

Keshava, Keshinisudana — Slayer of the Demon Keshi; Destroyer of Evil

Madhava — God of Fortune

Madhusudana — Slayer of Demon Madhu, i.e, Slayer of Ignorance

Mahatman — Sovereign Soul

Prabhu — Lord or Master

Prajapati — Divine Father of Countless Offspring

Purushottama — Supreme Spirit

Sahasrabaho — Thousand-armed

Varshneya — Scion of the Vrishni Clan

Vasudeva — Lord of the World; the Lord as Creator/Preserver/Destroyer

Vishnu — The All-pervading Preserver

Vishvamurte — Universe-bodied

Yadava — Descendant of Yadu

Yogeshvara — Lord of Yoga

Arjuna:

Anagha — *Sinless One*

Bharata — *Descendant of King Bharata*

Bharatashreshtha — *Best of the Bharatas*

Bharatarishabha — *Bull of the Bharatas, i.e., the best or most excellent of the descendants of the Bharata dynasty*

Bharatasattama — *Best of the Bharatas*

Dehabhritan Vara — *Supreme Among the Embodied*

Dhananjaya — *Winner of Wealth*

Gudakesha — *Conqueror of Sleep ("ever-ready, sleepless, delusion-defeating")*

Kaunteya — *Son of Kunti*

Kiritin — *Diademed One*

Kurunandana — *The Pride or Choice Son of the Kuru Dynasty*

Kurupravira — *Great Hero of the Kurus*

Kurusattama — *Flower (Best) of the Kurus*

Kurushreshtha — *Best of the Kuru Princes*

Mahabaho — *Mighty-armed*

Pandava — *Descendant of Pandu*

Parantapa — *Scorcher of Foes*

Partha — *Son of Pritha*

Purusharishabha — *Flower Among Men (lit., "bull" or chief among men)*

Purushavyaghra — *Tiger Among Men*

Savyasachin — *One Who Wields the Bow With Either Hand*

About the Author

"The ideal of love for God and service to humanity found full expression in the life of Paramahansa Yogananda....Though the major part of his life was spent outside India, still he takes his place among our great saints. His work continues to grow and shine ever more brightly, drawing people everywhere on the path of the pilgrimage of the Spirit."

—from a tribute by the Government of India upon issuing a commemorative stamp in Paramahansa Yogananda's honor on the twenty-fifth anniversary of his passing

Born in India on January 5, 1893, Paramahansa Yogananda devoted his life to helping people of all races and creeds to realize and express more fully in their lives the beauty, nobility, and true divinity of the human spirit.

After graduating from Calcutta University in 1915, Sri Yogananda took formal vows as a monk of India's venerable monastic Swami Order. Two years later, he began his life's work with the founding of a "how-to-live" school—since grown to twenty-one educational institutions throughout India—where traditional academic subjects were offered together with yoga training and instruction in spiritual ideals. In 1920, he was invited to serve as India's delegate to an International Congress of Religious Liberals in Boston. His address to the Congress and subsequent lectures on the East Coast were enthusiastically received, and in 1924 he embarked on a cross-continental speaking tour.

Over the next three decades, Paramahansa Yogananda contributed in far-reaching ways to a greater awareness and appreciation in the West of the spiritual wisdom of the East. In Los Angeles, he established an international headquarters for Self-Realization Fellowship—the nonsectarian religious society he had founded in 1920. Through his writings, extensive lecture tours, and the creation of numerous Self-Realization Fellowship temples and meditation centers, he introduced thousands of truth-seekers to the ancient science and philosophy of Yoga and its universally applicable methods of meditation.

Today, the spiritual and humanitarian work begun by Paramahansa Yogananda continues under the direction of Sri Daya Mata, one of his earliest and closest disciples and president of Self-Realization Fellowship/ Yogoda Satsanga Society of India since 1955. In addition to publishing his lectures, writings, and informal talks (including a comprehensive series of lessons for home study), the society also oversees its temples, retreats, and centers around the world; the monastic communities of the Self-Realization Order; and a Worldwide Prayer Circle.

In an article on Sri Yogananda's life and work, Dr. Quincy Howe, Jr., Professor of Ancient Languages at Scripps College, wrote: "Paramahansa Yogananda brought to the West not only India's perennial promise of God-realization, but also a practical method by which spiritual aspirants from all walks of life may progress rapidly toward that goal. Originally appreciated in the West only on the most lofty and abstract level, the spiritual legacy of India is now accessible as practice and experience to all who aspire to know God, not in the beyond, but in the here and now....Yogananda has placed within the reach of all the most exalted methods of contemplation."

The life and teachings of Paramahansa Yogananda are described in his *Autobiography of a Yogi* (see page 166).

Paramahansa Yogananda:
A Yogi in Life and Death

Paramahansa Yogananda entered *mahasamadhi* (a yogi's final conscious exit from the body) in Los Angeles, California, on March 7, 1952, after concluding his speech at a banquet held in honor of H. E. Binay R. Sen, Ambassador of India.

The great world teacher demonstrated the value of yoga (scientific techniques for God-realization) not only in life but in death. Weeks after his departure his unchanged face shone with the divine luster of incorruptibility.

Mr. Harry T. Rowe, Los Angeles Mortuary Director, Forest Lawn Memorial-Park (in which the body of the great master is temporarily placed), sent Self-Realization Fellowship a notarized letter from which the following extracts are taken:

"The absence of any visual signs of decay in the dead body of Paramahansa Yogananda offers the most extraordinary case in our experience....No physical disintegration was visible in his body even twenty days after death....No indication of mold was visible on his skin, and no visible desiccation (drying up) took place in the bodily tissues. This state of perfect preservation of a body is, so far as we know from mortuary annals, an unparalleled one....At the time of receiving Yogananda's body, the Mortuary personnel expected to observe, through the glass lid of the casket, the usual progressive signs of bodily decay. Our astonishment increased as day followed day without bringing any visible change in the body under observation. Yogananda's body was apparently in a phenomenal state of immutability....

"No odor of decay emanated from his body at any time....The physical appearance of Yogananda on March 27th, just before the bronze cover of the casket was put into position, was the same as it had been on March 7th. He looked on March 27th as fresh and as unravaged by decay as he had looked on the night of his death. On March 27th there was no reason to say that his body had suffered any visible physical disintegration at all. For these reasons we state again that the case of Paramahansa Yogananda is unique in our experience."

Additional Resources on the Kriya Yoga Teachings of Paramahansa Yogananda

Self-Realization Fellowship is dedicated to freely assisting seekers worldwide. For information regarding our annual series of public lectures and classes, meditation and inspirational services at our temples and centers around the world, a schedule of retreats, and other activities, we invite you to visit our website or our International Headquarters:

www.yogananda-srf.org

Self-Realization Fellowship
3880 San Rafael Avenue
Los Angeles, CA 90065
323 225-2471

SELF-REALIZATION FELLOWSHIP LESSONS

Personal guidance and instruction from Paramahansa Yogananda on the techniques of yoga meditation and principles of spiritual living

If you feel drawn to the spiritual truths described in *The Yoga of Jesus*, we invite you to enroll in the *Self-Realization Fellowship Lessons*.

Paramahansa Yogananda originated this home-study series to provide sincere seekers the opportunity to learn and practice the ancient yoga meditation techniques introduced in this book—including the science of *Kriya Yoga*. The *Lessons* also present his practical guidance for attaining balanced physical, mental, and spiritual well-being.

The *Self-Realization Fellowship Lessons* are available at a nominal fee (to cover printing and postage costs). All students are freely given personal guidance in their practice by Self-Realization Fellowship monks and nuns.

For more information...

Complete details about the *Self-Realization Fellowship Lessons* are included in the free booklet *Undreamed-of Possibilities*. To receive a copy of this booklet and an application form, please visit our website or contact our International Headquarters.

Also published by Self-Realization Fellowship...

AUTOBIOGRAPHY OF A YOGI

By Paramahansa Yogananda

This acclaimed autobiography presents a fascinating portrait of one of the great spiritual figures of our time. With engaging candor, eloquence, and wit, Paramahansa Yogananda narrates the inspiring chronicle of his life — the experiences of his remarkable childhood, encounters with many saints and sages during his youthful search throughout India for an illumined teacher, ten years of training in the hermitage of a revered yoga master, and the thirty years that he lived and taught in America. Also recorded here are his meetings with Mahatma Gandhi, Rabindranath Tagore, Luther Burbank, the Catholic stigmatist Therese Neumann, and other celebrated spiritual personalities of East and West.

Autobiography of a Yogi is at once a beautifully written account of an exceptional life and a profound introduction to the ancient science of Yoga and its time-honored tradition of meditation. The author clearly explains the subtle but definite laws behind both the ordinary events of everyday life and the extraordinary events commonly termed miracles. His absorbing life story thus becomes the background for a penetrating and unforgettable look at the ultimate mysteries of human existence.

Considered a modern spiritual classic, the book has been translated into more than twenty languages and is widely used as a text and reference work in colleges and universities. A perennial best seller since it was first published more than fifty years ago, *Autobiography of a Yogi* has found its way into the hearts of millions of readers around the world.

"A rare account." — THE NEW YORK TIMES

"A fascinating and clearly annotated study." — NEWSWEEK

"There has been nothing before, written in English or in any other European language, like this presentation of Yoga."

— COLUMBIA UNIVERSITY PRESS

OTHER BOOKS BY PARAMAHANSA YOGANANDA

Available at bookstores or directly from the publisher:
Self-Realization Fellowship
3880 San Rafael Avenue • Los Angeles, California 90065
Tel (323) 225-2471 • Fax (323) 225-5088
www.yogananda-srf.org

God Talks With Arjuna: *The Bhagavad Gita — A New Translation and Commentary*

In this monumental two-volume work, Paramahansa Yogananda reveals the innermost essence of India's most renowned scripture. Exploring its psychological, spiritual, and metaphysical depths, he presents a sweeping chronicle of the soul's journey to enlightenment through the royal science of God-realization.

The Second Coming of Christ: *The Resurrection of the Christ Within You — A revelatory commentary on the original teachings of Jesus*

In this unprecedented masterwork of inspiration, almost 1700 pages in length, Paramahansa Yogananda takes the reader on a profoundly enriching journey through the four Gospels. Verse by verse, he illumines the universal path to oneness with God taught by Jesus to his immediate disciples but obscured through centuries of misinterpretation: "how to become like Christ, how to resurrect the Eternal Christ within one's self."

Man's Eternal Quest

Paramahansa Yogananda's *Collected Talks and Essays* present in-depth discussions of the vast range of inspiring and universal truths that have captivated millions in his *Autobiography of a Yogi.* Volume I explores little-known and seldom-understood aspects of meditation, life after death, the nature of creation, health and healing, the unlimited powers of the mind, and the eternal quest that finds fulfillment only in God.

The Divine Romance
Volume II of Paramahansa Yogananda's collected talks and essays. Among the wide-ranging selections: *How to Cultivate Divine Love; Harmonizing Physical, Mental, and Spiritual Methods of Healing; A World Without Boundaries; Controlling Your Destiny; The Yoga Art of Overcoming Mortal Consciousness and Death; The Cosmic Lover; Finding the Joy in Life.*

Journey to Self-realization
Volume III of the collected talks and essays presents Sri Yogananda's unique combination of wisdom, compassion, down-to-earth guidance, and encouragement on dozens of fascinating subjects, including: *Quickening Human Evolution, How to Express Everlasting Youthfulness,* and *Realizing God in Your Daily Life.*

Wine of the Mystic: *The Rubaiyat of Omar Khayyam — A Spiritual Interpretation*
An inspired commentary that brings to light the mystical science of God-communion hidden behind the *Rubaiyat's* enigmatic imagery. Includes 50 original color illustrations. Winner of the 1995 Benjamin Franklin Award for best book in the field of religion.

Where There Is Light: *Insight and Inspiration for Meeting Life's Challenges*
Gems of thought arranged by subject; a unique handbook to which readers can quickly turn for a reassuring sense of direction in times of uncertainty or crisis, or for a renewed awareness of the ever present power of God one can draw upon in daily life.

Whispers from Eternity
A collection of Paramahansa Yogananda's prayers and divine experiences in the elevated states of meditation. Expressed in a majestic rhythm and poetic beauty, his words reveal the inexhaustible variety of God's nature, and the infinite sweetness with which He responds to those who seek Him.

The Science of Religion
Within every human being, Paramahansa Yogananda writes, there is one inescapable desire: to overcome suffering and attain a happiness that

does not end. Explaining how it is possible to fulfill these longings, he examines the relative effectiveness of the different approaches to this goal.

In the Sanctuary of the Soul: A Guide to Effective Prayer
Compiled from the works of Paramahansa Yogananda, this inspiring devotional companion reveals ways of making prayer a daily source of love, strength, and guidance.

Inner Peace: How to Be Calmly Active and Actively Calm
A practical and inspiring guide, compiled from the talks and writings of Paramahansa Yogananda, that demonstrates how we can be "actively calm" by creating peace through meditation, and "calmly active" — centered in the stillness and joy of our own essential nature while living a dynamic, fulfilling, and balanced life. Winner of the 2000 Benjamin Franklin Award — best book in the field of Metaphysics/Spirituality.

To Be Victorious in Life (How-to-Live Series)
In this powerful book, Paramahansa Yogananda shows how we can realize life's highest goals by bringing out the unlimited potential within us. He provides practical counsel for achieving success, outlines definite methods of creating lasting happiness, and tells how to overcome negativity and inertia by harnessing the dynamic power of our own will.

Why God Permits Evil and How to Rise Above It (How-to-Live Series)
Paramahansa Yogananda provides strength and solace for times of adversity by explaining the mysteries of God's *lila,* or divine drama. Readers will come to understand the reason for the dualistic nature of creation—God's interplay of good and evil—and receive guidance on how to rise above the most challenging of circumstances.

Living Fearlessly: Bringing Out Your Inner Soul Strength (How-to-Live Series)
Paramahansa Yogananda teaches us how to break the shackles of fear and reveals how we can overcome our own psychological stumbling blocks. *Living Fearlessly* is a testament to what we can become if we but have faith in the divinity of our true nature as the soul.

How You Can Talk With God
Defining God as both the transcendent, universal Spirit and the intimately personal Father, Mother, Friend, and Lover of all, Paramahansa Yogananda shows how close the Lord is to each one of us, and how He can be persuaded to "break His silence" and respond in a tangible way.

Metaphysical Meditations
More than 300 spiritually uplifting meditations, prayers, and affirmations that can be used to develop greater health and vitality, creativity, self-confidence, and calmness; and to live more fully in a conscious awareness of the blissful presence of God.

Scientific Healing Affirmations
Paramahansa Yogananda presents here a profound explanation of the science of affirmation. He makes clear why affirmations work, and how to use the power of word and thought not only to bring about healing but to effect desired change in every area of life. Includes a wide variety of affirmations.

Sayings of Paramahansa Yogananda
A collection of sayings and wise counsel that conveys Paramahansa Yogananda's candid and loving responses to those who came to him for guidance. Recorded by a number of his close disciples, the anecdotes in this book give the reader an opportunity to share in their personal encounters with the Master.

Songs of the Soul
Mystical poetry by Paramahansa Yogananda — an outpouring of his direct perceptions of God in the beauties of nature, in man, in everyday experiences, and in the spiritually awakened state of *samadhi* meditation.

The Law of Success
Explains dynamic principles for achieving one's goals in life, and outlines the universal laws that bring success and fulfillment — personal, professional, and spiritual.

Cosmic Chants: Spiritualized Songs for Divine Communion
Words and music to 60 songs of devotion, with an introduction explaining how spiritual chanting can lead to God-communion.

AUDIO RECORDINGS OF PARAMAHANSA YOGANANDA

- *Beholding the One in All*
- *Awake in the Cosmic Dream*
- *Songs of My Heart*
- *Be a Smile Millionaire*
- *The Great Light of God*
- *To Make Heaven on Earth*
- *One Life Versus Reincarnation*

- *Removing All Sorrow and Suffering*
- *In the Glory of the Spirit*
- *Follow the Path of Christ, Krishna, and the Masters*
- *Self-Realization: The Inner and the Outer Path*

OTHER PUBLICATIONS FROM SELF-REALIZATION FELLOWSHIP

The Holy Science by Swami Sri Yukteswar

Only Love: Living the Spiritual Life in a Changing World by Sri Daya Mata

Finding the Joy Within You: Personal Counsel for God-Centered Living by Sri Daya Mata

Enter the Quiet Heart: Creating a Loving Relationship With God by Sri Daya Mata

God Alone: The Life and Letters of a Saint by Sri Gyanamata

"Mejda": The Family and the Early Life of Paramahansa Yogananda by Sananda Lal Ghosh

Self-Realization (a quarterly magazine founded by Paramahansa Yogananda in 1925)

FREE INTRODUCTORY BOOKLET: *Undreamed-of Possibilities*

The scientific techniques of meditation taught by Paramahansa Yogananda, including *Kriya Yoga* — as well as his guidance on all aspects of balanced spiritual living — are taught in the *Self-Realization Fellowship Lessons*. For further information, please write for the free introductory booklet, *Undreamed-of Possibilities*.

———

A complete catalog describing all of the Self-Realization Fellowship publications and audio/video recordings is available on request.

AIMS AND IDEALS

OF

SELF-REALIZATION FELLOWSHIP

As set forth by Paramahansa Yogananda, Founder
Sri Daya Mata, President

To disseminate among the nations a knowledge of definite scientific techniques for attaining direct personal experience of God.

To teach that the purpose of life is the evolution, through self-effort, of man's limited mortal consciousness into God Consciousness; and to this end to establish Self-Realization Fellowship temples for God-communion throughout the world, and to encourage the establishment of individual temples of God in the homes and in the hearts of men.

To reveal the complete harmony and basic oneness of original Christianity as taught by Jesus Christ and original Yoga as taught by Bhagavan Krishna; and to show that these principles of truth are the common scientific foundation of all true religions.

To point out the one divine highway to which all paths of true religious beliefs eventually lead; the highway of daily, scientific, devotional meditation on God.

To liberate man from his threefold suffering: physical disease, mental inharmonies, and spiritual ignorance.

To encourage "plain living and high thinking"; and to spread a spirit of brotherhood among all peoples by teaching the eternal basis of their unity: kinship with God.

To demonstrate the superiority of mind over body, of soul over mind.

To overcome evil by good, sorrow by joy, cruelty by kindness, ignorance by wisdom.

To unite science and religion through realization of the unity of their underlying principles.

To advocate cultural and spiritual understanding between East and West, and the exchange of their finest distinctive features.

To serve mankind as one's larger Self.

Index